THE ART OF JUGGLING

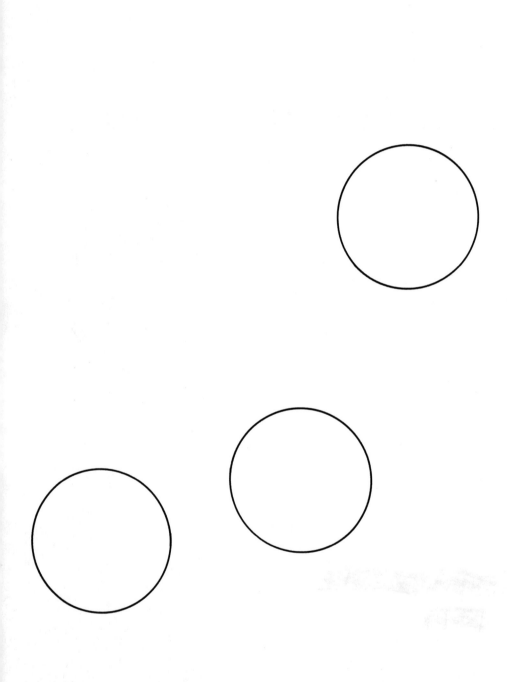

The Art Of JUGGLING

by Ken Benge

Published by
World Publications

Acknowledgements

I would like to thank Tom Henley for the illustrations, Carol Benge for the photographs and Jim Lilliefors for the editing of *The Art of Juggling*.

This book is dedicated to the International Jugglers Association.

CONTENTS

①THE END:
A False Stigma

"You never turned around to see the frowns on the jugglers and the clowns, when they all did tricks for you."

Bob Dylan, *Like A Rolling Stone*

Regardless of what your understanding of juggling might be, it is probably incomplete. The *Encyclopedia Americana* still tells people that juggling is "the dexterous manipulation of such objects as balls, plates, or Indian clubs." The *World Book* lists an additional usage of the word, "to describe the action of a person who tries to do something dishonest, especially with money."

Beneath the cloud of this sort of definition, juggling has lived for centuries as the world's most misunderstood sport, trapped in the stereotypes of circuses.

I have never been part of a circus, yet juggling has taken me from a point 16 years ago when I was literally afraid of life, to a position where I now have my own company, appear on television and at stage shows across the country. The idea that juggling requires some sort of special coordination or dexterity is one of the greatest fallacies surrounding the sport. Anyone can juggle. Perhaps everyone can't become a champion, or want to become a performer, but that's where we leave the stereotypes behind. Hopefully, we can now call an end to these false ideas.

I have spent more than half of my life juggling and in that time have found that the real values of the sport are the internal rewards it offers. Juggling has opened me up, taught me not only about my physical makeup, but about my mental makeup as well. The sense of accomplishment that came with each new trick gave me the confidence I so sorely lacked as a teenager. Even today, I can go to juggling for relief from the pressure of a difficult day at the office. A half hour of juggling can work wonders no drug will ever approach. It can heal feelings of inadequacy, boredom and self-consciousness.

But more than merely meditative or therapeutic, the greatest internal rewards involve creation. The prevailing idea in the minds of non-jugglers has long been that learning to juggle involves about as much creativity as painting by the numbers. Anyone who has juggled knows this isn't so. Once you have picked up the basic patterns, the natural inclination is always to experiment.

The ancient author Publilius Syrus wrote, "When two do the same thing, it is not the same thing after all." Though he probably wasn't thinking of juggling when he wrote it, it applies nevertheless. No two people juggle the same, even when doing identical patterns. They are always separated by their individuality, their personality. Once you move past the next chapter, you will already have developed your own unique style.

For me, juggling's greatest value is as a means of expression. And it is easily the cheapest and most accessible means available. You need no special props or facilities. You can learn it at home with erasers, rocks or golf balls. You can learn the art quickly too, as fast as an hour or less for the first basic pattern.

The invention and sense of worth that accompany juggling is valuable not only in itself, but also for the effect it will have on the rest of your life. When I began juggling as a teenager, it was a very private activity. I had no idea I would one day be doing it on national television for an audience of millions. Yet as my sense of confidence grew with my repertoire of tricks, both learned and invented, I experienced a strong urge to show what I had developed to others.

For years, perhaps because of our family's financial instability, I often seemed a notch below many of my peers. With juggling, I felt a new-found sense of worth. I was accomplishing something that demonstrated to me I was capable of achievement. I was doing something that other people weren't able to do. I literally juggled my way out of inferiority.

Most jugglers go through a similar process, though not necessarily to the same extent. Initially, they will practice alone, learning the basic patterns. Eventually, as their sense of accomplishment increases, they show their art to others.

Once you see it as art, as creation, you will find a whole new sense of value. As Emerson said, "Every genuine work of art has as much reason for being as the earth and the sun." When the juggler realizes this, he feels compelled to display, if only minimally, his work to others. By doing so, he has his sense of accomplishment (and in effect, his sense of worth) confirmed.

Once this confirmation occurs, the juggler's confidence grows. I am convinced that if I had never started juggling, I would not have more than a handful of the wealth and travel experience I own today. The confidence that has grown from my first juggling experience as a 12-year-old has taken me a long way.

My wife Carol has also gained in confidence through juggling. When I met her in a music class at San Diego State University, she was shy and somewhat withdrawn. The ability to juggle improved her confidence. She now juggles at shows and on television, and is a much more outgoing person.

Everywhere I go I see people who know how to do the basic juggling pattern but who, because of a lack of time or inclination, never will develop beyond it. I meet people who have always had a latent desire to learn at least the basic juggling patterns, but who don't know how to get started.

It has always bothered me that these people are just one small step away from discovering the unlimited world of juggling as art, and yet will probably never take that step. It has been difficult to blame them. There is no real impetus for them to advance, so they don't. Not only do they wonder the "how" of advancement, they also wonder the "why."

This book is intended as an answer to them, and an invitation to anyone else desiring to explore a new self-improving art. If you are able to push aside your preconceptions for an hour and give it a chance, juggling will change you.

Prior to my involvement with the sport, I also took the stereotypes for granted. But the second half of my life has altered that outlook. It now angers me to read the abundance of unfactual, generalized accounts in magazines, newspapers and other juggling books. Juggling has suffered long enough.

The very word "juggling" carries with it much of the problem. It stems from the Latin word *joculare*, meaning "to jest." The French equivalent, *jongleur*, was applied in medieval times to wandering minstrels who went from court to court singing songs or reading poetry. In the 14th century, jugglers fell into disrepute, and the bad connotations have lasted to the present.

In reality though, juggling pre-dates its name. It was practiced by the Egyptians, Greeks and Romans, and evidence of it is found in sculpture, coins and ancient manuscripts.

That juggling developed so long ago and has survived through today (despite this prevalent misunderstanding) is indicative of the symbolic implications it carries with it. More than any other sport or activity, juggling represents us and our plight as humans. We are, in effect, all jugglers, trying to keep more things than we can hold up in the air. Until we learn, we drop a few things. But once we learn, we evolve (through some failure and invention) to doing it with more complexity. The term "juggle things" turns up frequently in conversation but almost invariably has nothing to do with the sport, or art of juggling.

Perhaps the most reassuring aspect of juggling is the knowledge that once you learn it as an art, it will never run out on you. I still get the same thrill today from learning, or inventing, a new trick as I did 10 years ago.

I have heard many athletes talk about the pressures of achievement. You can never be satisfied, they claim, because no sooner have you crossed one hurdle than there is another one waiting for you, and you can never rest.

I have found that with juggling, unlike a hurdle race where you don't achieve satisfaction until you've crossed the final hurdle, you are able to relax after each achievement, yet still have the desire to accomplish more. There is no one timing you, there is no one fighting you, there is no pressure to do what you don't want to. Yet, at the same time, there is the personal challenge to keep you going.

I've included enough information in this book for you to take juggling anywhere you wish—to the point of making a career of it, and beyond. But unlike other authors I make no attempt to guide you, to tell you where you should take it. This guiding influence, which has occurred in practically all juggling literature, ignores the art, ignores the individuality that makes the sport what it is. This might be a suitable approach for teaching someone to become a circus juggler, but it is too restraining to allow the true potential of the sport to surface. In fact, if you just follow the tricks, you'll know enough by the end of the next two or three chapters to make a career in the circus. But I don't believe this is why you are reading the book.

I have seen children in the circus being taught to juggle. They are made to stand on a box and practice in front of their parents. Whenever they drop an object, they are hit. This is how they learn.

Juggling for them isn't fun. It isn't meditation. It isn't creation. It is discipline, pure and simple.

I've spent most of my life experiencing juggling as fun. I've developed much further than the circus clowns ever will yet I have never done it through discipline. I've learned that you accomplish much more when you let yourself enjoy it than when you force yourself to learn it.

One of my fellow juggling authors, Carlo, has said that juggling may very well become a national craze. As a discipline it never could. But as fun, as meditation and as art, the possibilities are limitless. Already it is catching on like never before. Among the list of famous faces who juggle are John Denver, Dick Van Dyke, Donny Osmond and Doug McClure. But more importantly, the list of non-famous faces is growing steadily as people begin to see how rewarding juggling can be.

It is not a sport that demands any special physique, like football, or any special equipment, like baseball, or any special environment, like skiing. And perhaps most importantly, it is not a sport that demands any special skills or preparation.

You are as ready as you ever will be right now, sitting in your chair reading this book. This is your personal invitation to discover for yourself the true benefits of juggling.

② THE CASCADE

The cascade is the basic juggling pattern. It is the first step in learning to juggle and serves as a base for further juggling patterns.

The procedure for learning the cascade will be discussed using balls, as will the rest of the patterns in the book. This is done for the sake of convenience, though I encourage using a wide variety of props in your juggling. I've devoted a whole chapter to props, so as you become more proficient you can refer to it for information on everything from batons to fire torches.

If you proceed through the steps for the cascade fully and patiently, you can learn how to juggle in very little time.

STEP ONE. Choose your juggling balls. The first of three considerations in finding yourself a good set of juggling balls is size. Although jugglers use a very wide range of sizes, I would recommend for your first set you find balls that will allow you to hold three in one hand comfortably.

For most people, the balls will be from 2¼-2½ inches in diameter.

Next you want to consider weight. This is something that many individuals ignore when beginning, but it is very important. When a juggling ball falls into your hand, the ball must have enough weight so that you can feel it. They should weigh somewhere between 4-6 ounces each. As you become more involved in juggling, you will begin to use different weights of balls to make certain patterns easier.

Your final consideration should be the color of the juggling balls. To control your juggling, you have to see the balls. Therefore, find balls that are painted or dyed a visible color. If you can't find them, you can dye or paint them yourself.

The most important step in learning to juggle is locating your imaginary points.

As you begin hunting for a good set of juggling balls, I would suggest three things. First, check large sporting good stores and ask if they have Canadian lacrosse balls. These make excellent juggling balls. Another suggestion is to check pet shops as there are several types of solid-rubber dog balls that work well for juggling. Finally, contact the International Jugglers Association for information on obtaining juggling balls. You can do this by writing me, in care of the publisher.

STEP TWO. Before even picking up your juggling balls, picture two imaginary points in the air. If you hold your hands straight up in the air from your shoulders, the two points will be about that high and out about six inches in front of your nose.

STEP THREE. Pick up one of your juggling balls in your right hand and place both of your hands in front of you, palms up, at waist level. Keep your eyes focused on the imaginary point that is above and in front of your left shoulder. Now, toss up the ball in the right hand with a 2-3 inch movement of your forearm and hand, throwing the ball to the imaginary point above and in front of the left shoulder. Then try to catch it with the left hand, making sure you do not watch your hand, but instead watch the ball as it starts down from the invisible point.

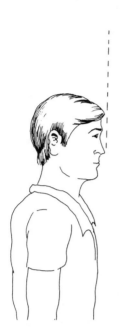

X

Imaginary points should be arm's length from the shoulders and about six inches out from your nose.

Stick the ball back in the right hand and try it until you can do it with ease. Make sure the peak of the flight is at the imaginary point which is on the left side, and do not watch your hands, but instead watch the imaginary points and the ball. Some students worry about how they catch the ball, or the position of the ball in the hand when it is thrown. To me there is no importance in the position as long as you throw it and catch it with ease.

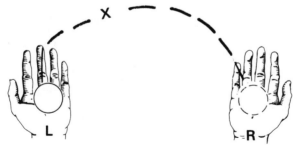

Ball should peak at the imaginary point.

STEP FOUR. Try starting with the ball in the left hand. This time throw it to the imaginary point above and in front of the right shoulder. In other words, the ball would start in the left hand, go up to the right imaginary point, then fall to the right hand.

Try it until you can do it with ease.

The Cascade

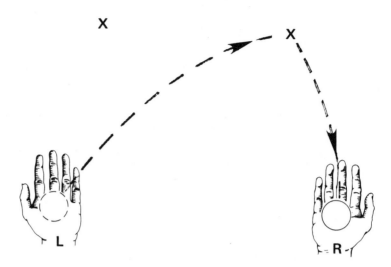

The ball is thrown from the left hand to the right imaginary point.

STEP FIVE. Put steps three and four together to begin proper preparation for three ball juggling. Start with one juggling ball in your right hand. Throw it to the left imaginary point, and as it falls catch it in the left hand. When you catch the ball in the left hand, let the hand drop two or three inches and then bring it back up and throw the ball to the right imaginary point. As it comes down from the right imaginary point, catch it in the right hand. Then the right hand drops slightly and again throws the ball to the left point, thus restarting the cycle.

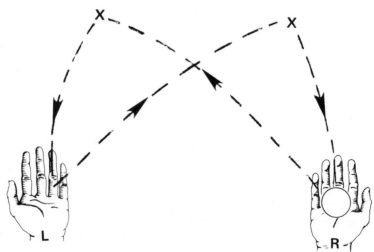

Steps three and four together.

The Art of Juggling

Practice throwing one ball around in this figure eight pattern. To many this will seem elementary, but remember it is the foundation for juggling three balls. And for some of you, the catching of the ball without looking at your hands will be difficult. Keep practicing, it will come.

STEP SIX. This is the two ball exchange which is one of the last building steps before you learn to juggle three balls.

Start with one ball in each hand. The object is to catch the balls in the opposite hands from which they were thrown. As the ball in the right hand corner is thrown and at the moment it gets to the left imaginary point, throw the ball in the left hand to the right imaginary point.

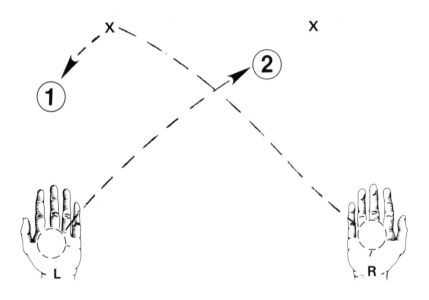

The left hand ball is thrown as soon as the right hand ball reaches the left imaginary point.

Notice that ball number two goes under ball number one, not over it.

There are three important things to remember while you are practicing this:

● Make sure you throw both balls to their imaginary points which are both the same height from your shoulders. In other words, throw both balls the same height in the air.

The Cascade

- Make sure your hands alternate throws. Throw your right hand ball. Wait for that ball to get up to its imaginary point and then throw the left hand ball.

- Only watch the balls while they are up near the imaginary points, not down by your hands.

After mastering the above two ball exchanges, try the same thing except instead of throwing the right hand ball first, throw the left hand ball first. Then stick both of these moves together. Throw right-left, left-right, right-left, etc. This move is your most important foundation for juggling three balls. Practice it until you are sure of it.

STEP SEVEN. Go back and review steps two through six.

STEP EIGHT. You are now ready to start work on the three-ball cascade. To begin, place two balls (1 & 2) in your right hand and one ball (3) in your left hand. The object is to throw ball number one (1) from the right hand to the left imaginary point.

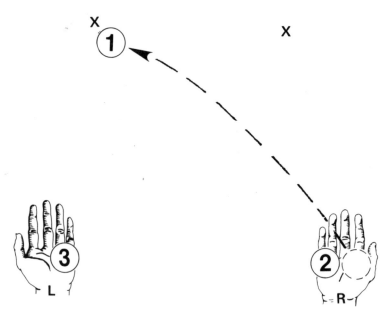

The start of the three ball cascade.

When it gets there, you throw the ball in your left hand (3) to the right imaginary point.

The Art of Juggling

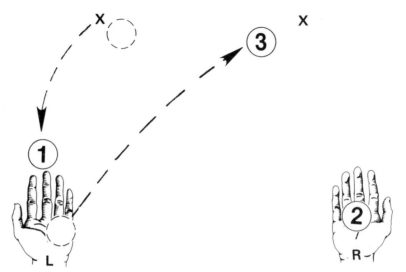

As ball number one drops, number three reaches the right imaginary point.

Then catch ball number one in the left hand. (So far, this is the same as the two ball exchange you mastered in step six. You are simply throwing the first ball number one up to the left imaginary point, when it gets there, you throw the left hand ball number three under number one to the right imaginary point.)

Now, as ball number three reaches the right imaginary point, you throw ball number two (2) from your right hand to the left imaginary point.

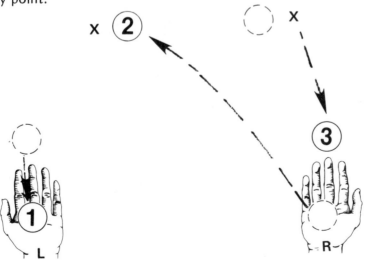

Ball number two is thrown when number three reaches the right imaginary point.

And then catch the falling ball (3) in your right hand. Again, this is a repeat of step six; you are throwing the left hand ball (3) to the right imaginary point. And when it gets there you are throwing the right hand ball (2) under it, up to the left imaginary point.

So, to go over the whole process to this point, throw ball number one from the right hand to the left imaginary point. When it gets there, you throw ball number three from your left hand up to your right imaginary point. And, when it (3) gets there, throw ball number two from your right hand to the left imaginary point.

If you have thrown the balls to the proper points, in the proper sequence, and your hands have continued to catch them, at this point you are re-starting the cycle. In other words, a ball (2) will be at the left hand imaginary point, beginning its downward path to the left hand. So, your left hand throws the ball it is holding (1) up to the right imaginary point. Next, your right hand throws the ball (3) it is holding up to the left imaginary point, and so on. And, once you can keep the cycle going you will be doing the cascade juggle.

At this point, before practicing any further, go back and re-read the three points to keep in mind in step six, and also keep these things in mind while you are practicing at this point.

As you continue working on the three ball cascade, make sure that each consecutive ball goes underneath the one thrown before it. It might take you a week or two of practice to keep the three-ball cascade under control. So at first, just try and keep it going as long as possible. And if you find yourself walking and throwing the balls forward and away from yourself, the solution is to keep practicing and keep trying to throw the balls back to the imaginary points. Also, don't worry about learning to stop your cascade juggling cycle. Stopping the balls will come automatically after you can keep the cycle going.

Once you can keep the cycle going for more than ten or fifteen seconds, try juggling while you are walking forward and back, running, or turning around. This practice will help you gain better control of your juggling before you begin working on the tricks in the following chapters.

The Art of Juggling

③ BEGINNING PATTERNS

This first section of tricks is designed to help you gain full control over your juggling and at the same time give you some showy tricks. These patterns look very professional but can be learned quickly.

ONE HIGH

As you are juggling, throw one ball up about 10 feet in the air and as it comes down start juggling.

Even though this is a simple trick, non-jugglers always like to see a juggler do it. As you are juggling, wait until a ball is in your right hand. When it gets there, throw it 8-10 feet straight up in the air. Be careful not to throw it out in front of you.

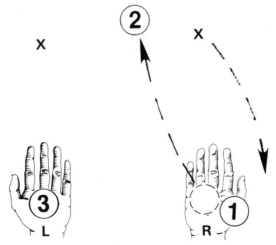

Ball number two goes 8-10 feet straight up in the air.

As it is going up, catch the other two balls, one in the left hand and one in the right. As the ball in the air comes down to the left hand and approximately passes your left imaginary point, throw the ball in the left hand to the right imaginary point and then catch the ball that is coming down.

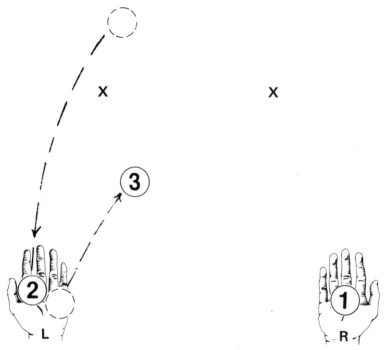

As ball number two descends, throw number three to the right imaginary point.

This again puts you into the basic cascade juggle.

Another trick, which is an adaptation of this, is to let the ball fall past your hands as it comes down, letting it bounce on the ground. After it bounces, let the ball continue up to the left imaginary point and this again puts you back into the cascade pattern.

THREE HIGH

Throw all three balls high, wait for them to come down and then start juggling again.

To do this trick, simply plot a new set of imaginary points, eight to ten feet straight above your old points. Then as you are juggling to the height of your regular points throw a ball, when it gets to your right hand, up to the new left imaginary point. Almost as soon as you throw the right ball, a ball will land in your left hand. Take the left

The Art of Juggling

hand ball and throw it up to the new right imaginary point. And again, almost as soon as you throw this one, another ball will be in your right hand. Throw this ball high to your new left imaginary point.

At this point all three balls should be up in the air. As they come down, catch them one at a time in their respective hands and throw them back into the cascade pattern at its regular height. If all three balls seem to be arriving back to your hands at the same time, it is because you are not throwing all of the balls the same height in the air.

After you become proficient at this, try clapping your hands together while the balls are up in the air. Many jugglers can get up to three claps before the balls come back to their hands.

REVERSE CASCADE

To someone watching you do this juggling trick, it appears that the balls are going over the top and dropping down into the center between the other balls.

Remember that in the basic cascade you threw a ball up, then the next ball went under it. In the reverse cascade, after you throw the first ball, the next one goes up and over it then drops into the other hand.

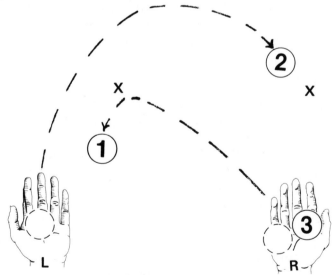

The reverse cascade.

Once you get to this point in the trick you are back to the beginning of the cycle. Just keep it going.

ONE UNDER YOUR LEG

Right Leg. As you are juggling, raise your right leg and throw a ball under it with your right hand.

This sounds easy but will take practice. There is a rhythm with which you bring up the right leg and throw the ball in the right hand under the leg. This rhythm is something that you must develop for yourself. However, here are some hints that will help you to find the rhythm.

First, try starting the cascade juggle by throwing your first ball in the right hand (which holds two) under your leg up to the left imaginary point and then start juggling. This will help develop your timing to get back into the juggle once the ball goes under your leg.

Second, it is important that when you throw the ball from your right hand under the leg, that you throw it to your left imaginary point and then catch it in your left hand. When you try the trick from a basic cascade, this crossing pattern will keep the basic cascade in motion, even though you are going under your leg.

Left Leg. As you are juggling, raise your left leg, throw a ball under it and continue juggling.

While you are juggling, and a ball gets to your left hand, raise your left leg and throw a ball under it to the right imaginary point. This then puts you back into the cascade pattern. This trick will probably be harder to learn than under your right leg but it will come with practice. And, while you are learning this trick, be sure to keep practicing under your right leg also.

TWO IN ONE HAND

This can be done with either hand. However, if you are right handed you should start by learning how to do two in your right hand.

Start with just one ball and think about the imaginary point above your right hand. Try to throw the ball in a circular motion so that at the top of its flight it hits the imaginary point.

It is very important that you keep the circular flight pattern of the ball parallel to the body, *not* at a right angle. Practice throwing one ball until you can do it with ease. You will probably have a tendency to make its flight pattern look like a football standing on end. Work to make the ball curve around in a clockwise circle (counter clockwise if you are doing it left handed).

To get both balls going in one hand, throw the first one out in its circular pattern and when that ball gets to the right imaginary point,

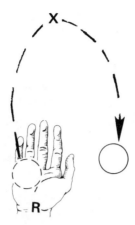

The flight pattern should look like a football standing on end.

throw out the second ball in the same circular pattern. Next, catch the first one and again re-throw it out when the second ball reaches the imaginary point.

Once you master the trick with one hand, learn it with the other.

There is another way to do two balls in one hand: simply throw the balls straight up and down. The timing is exactly the same as for the last method, except that you do not throw the balls in a circle.

Notice that balls one and two never crossed, they went straight up and down. As you are practicing this method, be sure to throw both balls the same height in the air.

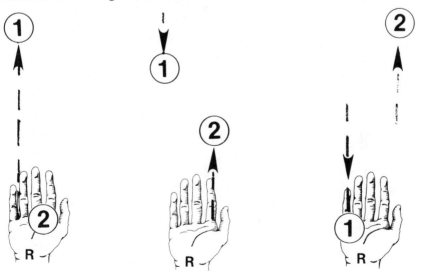

Balls one and two are thrown straight up and down.

The next two tricks will require your ability to do both of these moves.

ONE CENTER, TWO OUT

In this trick, one ball goes up and down in the center as two others go up and down in unison on the outside of the center one.

This trick involves juggling two balls in the right hand in a non-circular pattern and the third ball in the left hand.

Ball number one is thrown up in the center.

As ball number one starts to come down, the other two are thrown up on either side.

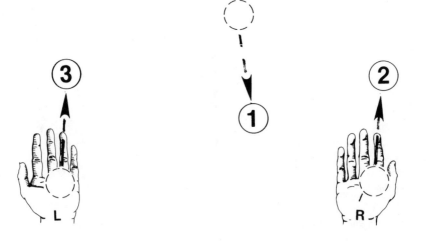

The Art of Juggling

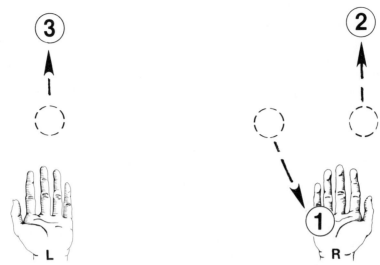

Balls two and three should be in unison.

From this point, catch ball number one in your right hand and again throw it back up in the center.

Balls number two and three will be coming down together, so you can catch them in unison and again throw them back up on the outside.

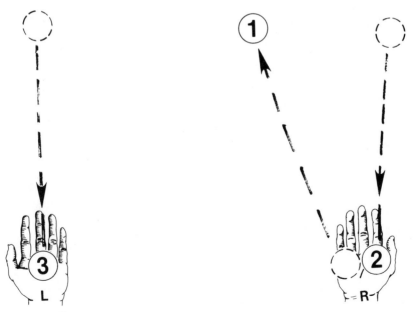

Ball number one is thrown as numbers two and three drop.

Once you have mastered this with the right hand, try having the left hand work two balls and let the right hand work one.

Another variation of this trick that looks the same but develops different skills, is to alternate throwing the middle ball with your right and left hands.

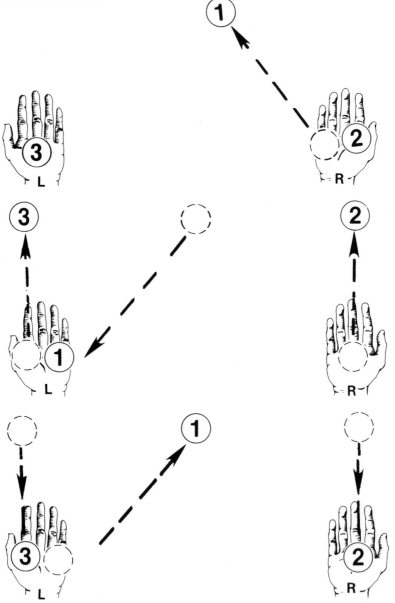

The sequence for alternately throwing the middle ball with right and left hands.

The Art of Juggling

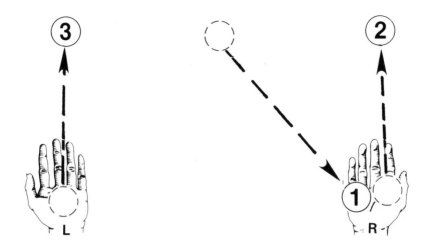

Notice that balls number two and three go straight up and down in unison and ball number one always stays in the middle, it is just caught by a different hand each time.

The final variation of this is the "crossover." Whenever you see a juggler do this, you will see the "one center, two out" move done first. As he gets into the trick, the two outside balls cross over the center so that they change hands. The center ball's flight pattern remains unchanged.

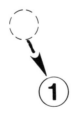

Balls two and three are held until number one begins to fall.

As ball number one starts to descend, balls number two and three are thrown up in the air in a crossing pattern so that they change sides.

Beginning Patterns

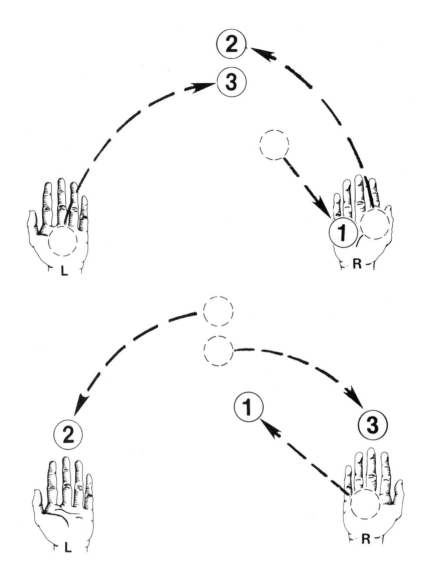

Balls two and three change sides as number one is thrown out.

The major problem you will probably encounter with this trick is having balls number two and three hit at the top when you try to exchange them. To prevent this you have to throw one ball just a little higher than the other.

If you get so you can do the exchange without hitting, try hitting the balls on purpose, thus causing them to bounce back to the hands they came from.

ONE AROUND YOUR BACK

As you are juggling, throw a ball around your back.

As it comes from behind your back to the front, continue juggling. This is a standard move most seasoned jugglers can do with ease. However, learning it will take practice.

To begin, wait until a ball is in your right hand, then with a quick motion, throw it around your back and up over your left shoulder to your left imaginary point. Then immediately move your right hand back into a normal juggling position and catch the ball that is dropping to that position. In the meantime the ball that you threw around behind your back is beginning to drop to your left hand. So, throw the ball that your left hand is holding to your right imaginary point and catch the downcoming ball. This will put you back into a normal cascade pattern.

As you are trying the above, you will find it to be a difficult move at first. To make it easier, try the following:

● Start with only one ball in your right hand and throw it in the desired flight pattern behind your back. Develop your throws and flight pattern so that you know where to throw the ball with your right hand and more important, where your left hand is going to catch the ball.

● Slow down your juggling cascade pattern before throwing one behind your back. This gives your right hand more time to throw the ball behind your back and then get in front to catch the next ball.

If you have trouble with this trick, don't worry. It will take time.

ONE OVER SHOULDER

A ball from your right hand is thrown behind your back and up over your right shoulder to the front right imaginary point.

As the ball descends to your right hand, continue your regular cascade juggle.

This trick is similar to "one around your back" in timing, but the ball is thrown and caught with the same hand. After the right hand throws the ball over the right shoulder it will immediately have to come back in front to catch the other ball that is dropping to it. As soon as you do so you will have to throw it to the left imaginary point so that you can then catch the ball that went over your shoulder. If you have followed the moves to this point, you are now back into a basic cascade pattern.

Something that will help you with this move is practicing first

A ball is thrown over your right shoulder to the front right imaginary point.

with just one ball. Throw the ball from your right hand, over your right shoulder, catch it in the right hand. If you keep this up it will do two things.

● It will help your arm develop the ability to throw the ball over your shoulder.

● And it will probably make your muscles sore for a day or so. Don't worry, the sore muscles will go away as you practice and develop.

OVER HEAD WITH ONE-HALF TURN

Throw a ball two or three feet over your head, so that it drops on your backside. As the ball is doing this, make a half turn toward the back and continue juggling.

This is an impressive looking juggling trick and yet it only requires a few days of practice. As you are juggling, your right hand throws a ball two or three feet up from and over your head. As the ball goes over, your head and eyes simply follow it as your body slowly turns counter-clockwise and your hands (with the two other balls) resume the cascade pattern of juggling.

DOUBLE SHOWER

In this trick the balls thrown from the right hand go over the balls thrown from the left. Therefore, all the balls thrown from the left hand always go under those thrown by the right.

Another way of doing this trick is to wait until a ball arrives in your right hand, then throw that ball outside and over the top of the other balls in the air. That is the basic pattern that the balls thrown from the right hand must take. Keep doing the same throw with each ball that hits your right hand. But remember, the left hand keeps throwing all of its balls in the normal cascade pattern.

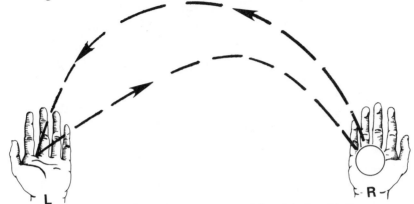

The basic double shower pattern with a right hand ball.

Finally, one other way of analyzing the same trick. Your left hand is doing the normal cascade as the right hand is doing the reverse cascade.

THE SHOWER

If you have ever looked at a picture of a comic-strip character juggling, you may recall that the balls were being juggled in a circular motion. This is called the shower pattern. Many people first learn to juggle by using the shower. However, it is harder than the cascade because it requires faster hand actions.

If you follow the pattern of one ball, it starts in the right hand, goes up in the air, and falls into the left hand. The left hand throws the ball sideways, straight across to the right hand.

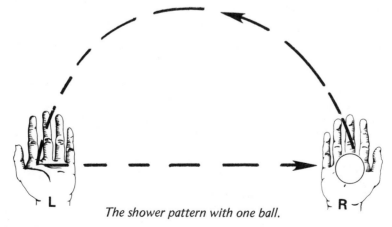

The shower pattern with one ball.

Try throwing one ball in this pattern. It is important when you are learning the trick to throw the balls up to the height of your imaginary points, although not directly to either of them. Also notice that the balls move in a counter-clockwise circle.

After you can throw one ball in the pattern, pick up two balls and place them both in your right hand. Throw out ball number one in the above pattern and then, as it gets to the top of its flight, throw out ball number two in the same pattern.

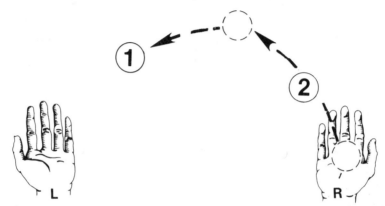

Ball number two is thrown out as soon as number one gets to the top of its flight.

As soon as ball number one drops to the left hand, immediately throw it sideways straight across to the right hand.

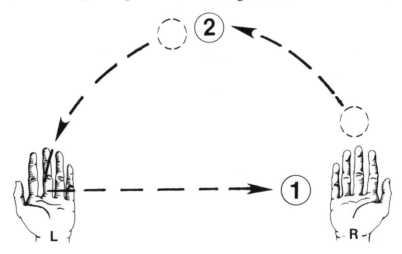

Pattern for the shower with two balls.

As soon as ball number one arrives in your right hand, ball number two will land in the left. Catch it, and then immediately throw out ball number one in the circular pattern again. And, immediately after you do that, throw ball number two sideways straight across to the right hand. Keep both balls going in the same circular pattern.

When you are ready to try the pattern with three balls, start by placing two balls in your right hand and one in your left. Now, with great speed, individually throw out the two in the right hand in the circular pattern.

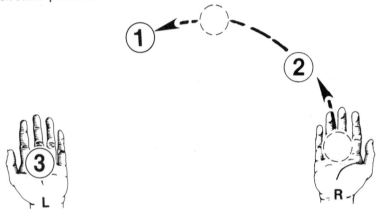

Ball number three is held until number two is thrown.

As soon as ball number two leaves your right hand, throw ball number three sideways straight across to your right hand.

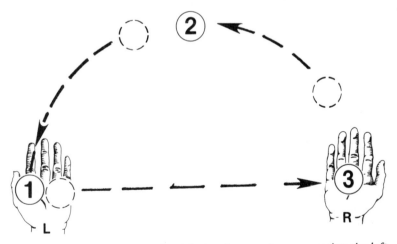

Ball three should arrive at the right hand as number one reaches the left.

Now catch ball number one in the left hand, throw ball number three in the circular pattern, and then number one sideways straight across.

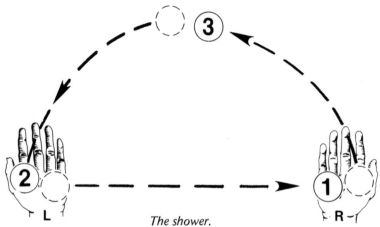

The shower.

You now have the shower pattern in motion, it's just a matter of keeping it going.

Once you master the counter-clockwise shower, try it clockwise. The pattern would be the same except the balls would be thrown from the left hand up in the air, the right hand would catch them and pass them sideways straight across to the left hand.

OVERHAND JUGGLING

The balls seem to be snatched right out of the air by your hands. In actuality, you are juggling using the basic cascade pattern except that your hands are turned over (palms down) throwing and catching the balls from the top instead of underneath.

The easiest way to learn this trick is with one ball. Place both of your hands palm down and hold the ball in your right hand.

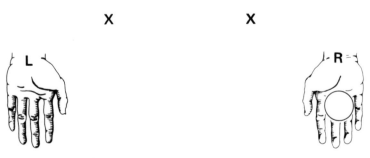

Starting position for overhand juggling.

The object is to raise up your right hand and arm and throw the ball to the left imaginary point. Then as the ball comes down, your left hand, palm down, moves up over the ball and then with a quick downward movement catches it. The ball is going through the basic cascade pattern except that your hands are palm down instead of palm up.

After you can throw and catch one ball easily, try using two balls and the basic cascade pattern. After doing it with two, try three. When first learning to do it with three, start off with your palms down. But as you become more proficient, start juggling using the basic cascade and then turn your hands over and continue juggling with the overhand movement.

Beginning Patterns

④ STOPPING AND STARTING

If you have learned any of the tricks in the last chapter, you're already able to stop and start. But doing it with a flourish makes your juggling much more interesting and polished.

BASIC STARTS

One Under Leg. Throw the first ball under your right leg and then start juggling.

Over Shoulder. Throw the first ball that you normally start your juggle with over your right shoulder and then start juggling.

Around Your Back. Throw one ball around your back and then begin your juggle.

TWO AROUND BACK

Your right hand throws two balls around behind your back. As the balls come up over your left shoulder and fall in front, start juggling.

There are two important things in learning this start. First, you must know how to throw the balls so they go around your shoulder in a neat, orderly pattern. Second, you must learn how to start juggling once they come from behind your back.

When you hold the balls it is important that you hold both of them in the same hand, but they must be held separately. When I am doing this trick, I hold one ball with my thumb, forefinger, and second finger. The other ball I hold within the palm of my hand, with the third and little fingers. With this individual grip I can release either ball with independent control.

Another important factor in controlling the flight pattern of the balls is to keep the back of your hand parallel to the floor while you are throwing the balls around your back.

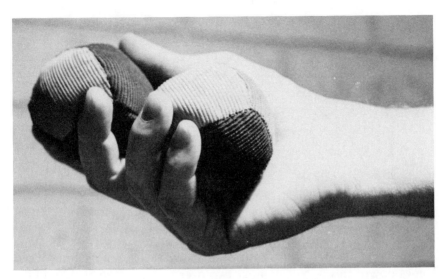

Hold one ball with your thumb, forefinger and second finger, and the other in your palm.

In order to start your basic cascade juggle, throw ball number three (which you have been holding in your left hand) between balls number one and two. As soon as you do this, you will catch ball number two in your right hand and then ball number one in your left hand.

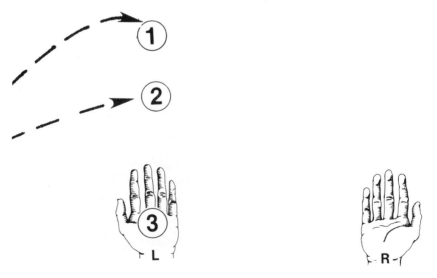

Ball number three is held until numbers one and two come around your back.

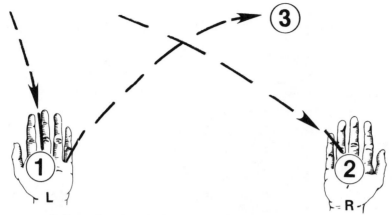

Ball number three is thrown between numbers one and two.

Now you are back into your basic cascade. As ball number three comes down, throw ball number two over to the left imaginary point and keep juggling.

THREE BOUNCE

Holding three balls in your right hand, throw them down to the ground and then as they bounce up, catch them and begin to juggle.

The first thing to learn in this trick is the manner in which you hold the three balls in your right hand. This is important for maintaining control of the balls for this start, as well as the next two starts.

Ball number one is held between the thumb and first finger. Ball number two is held between the first finger, second finger and third finger. Ball number three is held against the palm of the hand by pressure from the little finger.

The proper grip for holding three balls in your right hand.

The Art of Juggling

To learn to bounce the balls, hold them well spaced as shown in the picture and then turn your palm down. With your palm down and parallel to the floor, make a smooth fast downward motion, releasing the balls. This sends the balls down evenly and horizontally, avoiding a collision as they hit the floor. After the balls hit the floor all at once, they all come bouncing up together.

This brings us to the second part of the trick, catching the balls and re-starting the cascade. As you are first releasing the balls when throwing them down, notice that your right arm and hand are extended down toward the balls. Try bouncing all of the balls again but this time have both your right and left arms extended stiffly down toward the balls, palms down.

When all three of the balls come up toward your two extended arms, catch numbers one and three with your palms down. Ball number two should continue on up if you have bounced the balls hard enough and if you have balls that bounce well. Let ball number two continue up as you bring your hands to their normal juggling position.

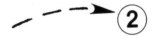

Balls one and three are caught as number two drops to the right hand.

As ball number two drops to the right hand, simply throw ball number three to the left imaginary point. This puts you into the normal cascade pattern.

THREE UNDER LEG

Three balls held in your right hand are thrown under your right leg whereupon you go straight into a cascade juggle.

To start, hold the three balls in your right hand in the same manner you did for the three bounce start. With the balls in that position, and your palms up (keeping the palm of your hand parallel with the floor), throw the three balls under your right leg.

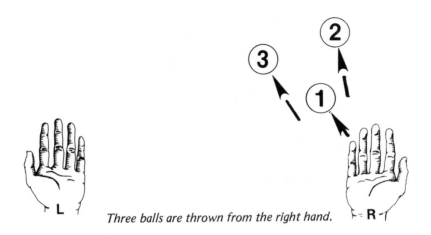

Three balls are thrown from the right hand.

When you throw the balls under your leg, give them enough thrust so that they will go up in the air past your imaginary points. Once they pass the imaginary points, your hands reach up simultaneously and grab balls number one and three with your palms down.

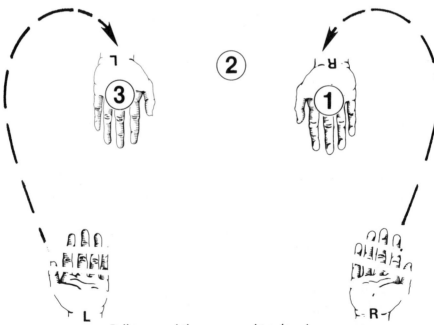

Balls one and three are caught palms down.

As the hands grab balls number one and three they must continue down and turn back over. If all of this is done in haste, ball number two should still be up in the air.

The Art of Juggling

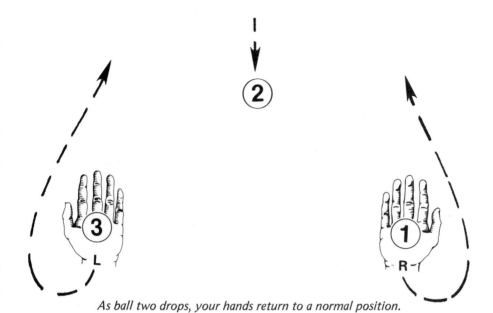

As ball two drops, your hands return to a normal position.

You are now in a position to start your three ball cascade pattern. Simply throw ball number one to the left imaginary point and catch ball number two in your right hand.

THREE AROUND BACK

The three balls held in the right hand are thrown around your back and over your left shoulder into a normal cascade pattern.

This trick is the same as the last one except you throw the balls around your back and over your shoulder instead of under your leg. The same basic two things are important. One, you must hold the balls correctly in the right hand. Two, you must grab two of the balls out of the air just as you did in the three under your leg start.

THREE OVER SHOULDER

The three balls held in the right hand are thrown over your right shoulder into a normal cascade pattern.

Again, this trick requires the same general moves as the last two, however, I believe this trick is harder than the last ones, so you may have to try it a few more times.

BEHIND BACK CATCH

As you finish your juggling, throw a ball up and over your shoulder and catch it behind your back.

From a cascade juggle in front of you, throw a ball from your right hand up in the air and over your left shoulder. As the ball is going up, your right hand catches the next ball that is coming to it and then the right hand quickly places the ball over into the left hand, so that the left hand now contains two balls. Now the right hand quickly swings around behind your back and catches the ball that is coming down behind your left shoulder.

The left hand ball is caught with the right hand.

This trick will require practice. If you throw the ball up a little higher than you normally throw it, and watch it closely with your eyes, you will soon be able to catch it.

UNDER LEG CATCH

While juggling, throw one ball up and over to your left side. As the ball falls down toward the ground, your right hand reaches through your legs toward your back left side. With your legs bent slightly, your right hand catches the dropping ball.

This is a really nice finish for a routine. Start with one ball and try throwing it parallel, and slightly to the left of your body. As the ball is dropping, your right hand goes between your slightly spread legs and catches the falling ball.

The Art of Juggling

There are three things to do while working on this trick. First, after you throw the ball up and over to your left, your right hand must catch a ball and place it in your left hand before you can have that hand free to go through your legs and catch the dropping ball. Second, do not take your feet off the floor. Third, you must bend your legs and body down in order to get your right hand far enough over to the left to catch the ball.

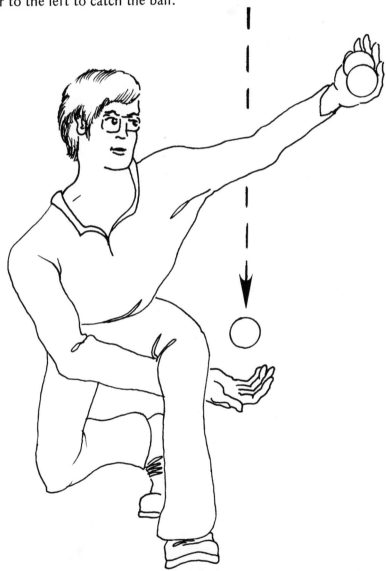

Bend your legs and catch the ball with your right hand under your left leg.

Stopping and Starting

NECK CATCH

While juggling, throw a ball up above your head and as the ball is coming down, lean and crouch forward to catch it on the back of your neck.

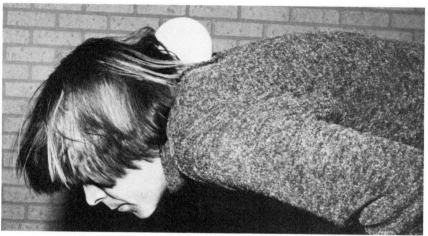

Neck catch.

In the above picture, you can see where the ball must land. However, in order to keep it there you must learn to form an impression, or valley, for the ball to sit in. You do this by making sure your head is tilted up as far as it can go, while you are also keeping your back slanted down toward your head. The valley is formed between your slanted head and slanted back.

The Art of Juggling

If you try the trick as I have described it to this point, you will soon realize two more things. First, as the ball drops and you try to catch it behind your neck, you must let your legs and body give with the trick. Second, you will need to keep your shoulder blades up, so the ball won't roll sideways.

Once you learn to catch the ball behind your neck you can get the ball back into the air with the snap of your neck, thus putting it in a position to catch it. Or, by simply standing up straight once you catch the ball behind your neck, you can cause the ball to roll down your back so that a hand placed behind your back can catch the ball.

NECK AND SHOULDER CATCH

A ball is thrown from your right hand up close to your left ear. When it gets up between your left shoulder and cheek, catch it.

Neck and shoulder catch.

When first learning this, practice with just one ball. Throw the ball so that it almost rolls up your chest to your left shoulder. Once it gets to your shoulder, catch it between your cheek bone and shoulder by making a fast upward motion with your left shoulder, thus pinching the ball between the side of your head and your shoulder.

This move is one that will require a great deal of practice if you are going to do it accurately. And, the kind of collar on your shirt will also make a difference.

CHIN CATCH

A ball *placed* by the right hand under your chin is pinched and held there between your chin and chest.

To get back into your juggle, your left hand throws the ball it is holding to the right imaginary point. Then the left hand reaches up and grabs the ball under the chin, thus putting you back into the cascade pattern.

After you have mastered one "chin catch," try doing them continuously. This can be a very funny juggling move.

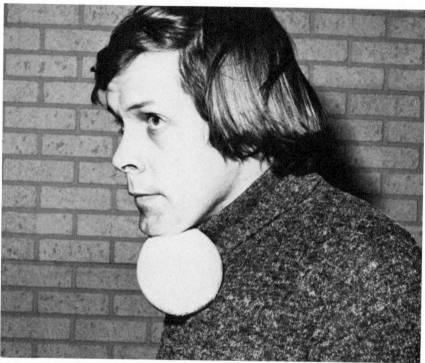

This is how you start the chin catch.

FOOT CATCH

A ball is dropped down and caught on your right foot. This one is difficult and requires hours of practice.

First, I will tell you about the basic principle of the trick. Stand on your left leg and hold your right foot, without any shoes, out in front of you. Point your foot so it lines up with your right leg.

With your foot and leg in that position, bend all of your toes up as far as they can go. This will form a pocket. It is in this pocket that the ball is caught. It is in this pocket that the ball sits.

The Art of Juggling

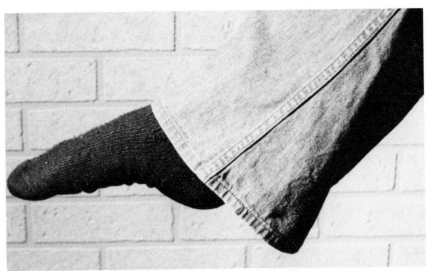

Extend your leg for the foot catch.

Now you know the basic principle of the trick. However, it will still require hours and hours of practice. One method of practice that may help is to let the ball bounce on the ground before you try to catch it in the pocket. Another thing that may help is to set the ball on your foot and just try holding it there. These different hints for working on the balance will help you gain an understanding of the trick. But, the trick itself will still require hours of practice.

Catch the ball in the pocket formed by bending your toes.

ONE HIGH WITH PIROUETTE

At the end of a juggle you throw one ball four or five feet up in the air. While it is in the air, you quickly turn a pirouette and catch the ball before it hits the ground.

There are several ways to turn your body around gracefully. Pivot on your left foot. With your weight on your left leg, give a hard push with your right foot to get your body to turn around. Your body should move counter-clockwise during its revolution.

After you can do the turn gracefully by itself, try it with one ball. Throw the ball up in the air, then turn your body once around very quickly and catch it. When you can do it fairly accurately with one ball, try it out of a three ball juggle. To accomplish this you would throw one ball up, then as you start your pirouette, your right hand catches the ball coming to it and quickly puts that ball into the left hand which already holds one ball. This action leaves your right hand free to catch the remaining ball after your turn. It is important to make the motion of placing the right hand ball into the left hand a graceful part of the pirouette.

If you wish to use the "one high pirouette" as a trick in a routine, as opposed to a stop, try throwing one high, turn, and then continue your juggle. This would be the same as "one high" except you turn while the ball is in the air.

⑤ INTERMEDIATE PATTERNS

I have made no attempt to describe all of the possible patterns in juggling. There are far too many, more than I even know of. The tricks in this chapter are more challenging than previous ones and should encourage you to develop some on your own.

THE INVISIBLE STRING

When someone sees you doing this trick, it will appear to them that one ball is being held in the juggle by an invisible string. Actually, this trick combines two things. First, your right hand simply juggles two balls using the straight up and down method. Secondly, your left hand simply holds the extra ball (number three) and makes a straight up and down movement, in unison with ball number one.

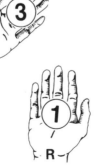

Ball number three remains in the left hand as numbers one and two are juggled in the right.

Presuming that you can do a controlled "two balls in one hand" using the straight up and down method, concentrate on the action of the left hand. First, hold the extra ball throughout the trick, with your left hand about two or three inches above the inside right hand ball.

The inside right ball (number one) is down. As you throw it straight up, raise your left hand holding ball number three straight up two or three inches above ball number one.

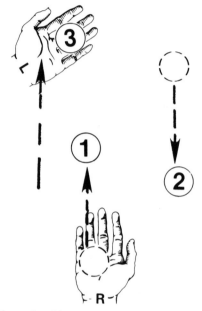

Ball number three should rise two or three inches above number one.

This raising of ball number three should be done in tempo and at the same speed as ball number one's throw up from the right hand. To keep the trick going, always keep ball number three, held tightly in your left hand, two to three inches above ball number one as ball number one goes up and down in its pattern. When you begin to show this move to your relatives or friends, be sure you hold the ball in the left hand so that it is visible, face on, to the person watching you.

ONE BALL THROUGH TWO

As you are doing two balls in your right hand, the left hand (holding the extra ball) keeps moving horizontally back and forth through the juggle.

The Art of Juggling

I use the circular pattern for the two balls in one hand. However, I have seen other jugglers do it using the straight up and down pattern. So, use the pattern that feels best for you.

The basic idea of the pattern is to wait until you throw a ball to the right imaginary point. At this time, move your left hand straight across horizontally through the two ball juggle.

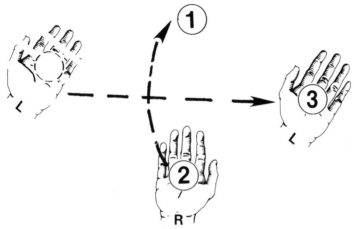

The left hand moves straight across as ball number one reaches the right imaginary point.

As soon as you throw ball number two up to the top of its flight, bring the left hand back through the two-ball juggle in the right hand.

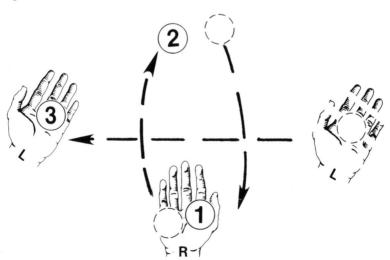

The left hand returns to position through the two-ball juggle.

Intermediate Patterns

If you go back over the explanation of this trick, you will see that I have placed emphasis on watching balls one or two at the top of their flight. This is the whole key to the trick. If you have trouble finding the proper timing to make this pattern work, try figuring the rhythm out with only one ball in the right hand. Throw the one ball up, move your left hand through, catch the ball and then re-throw it up, move the left hand back through, and then repeat the whole sequence.

To keep it all going, just keep the left hand moving steadily back and forth through the right hand juggle.

ONE BALL AROUND

As you are doing two balls in your right hand, the left hand (holding the third ball) keeps circling around each of the right hand balls as they reach the top of their flight.

It is important in this trick that you juggle the balls in your right hand in a circular pattern. Then, as you start to throw ball number one from your right hand, your left hand (holding ball number three) starts to make a circular pattern around your right imaginary point.

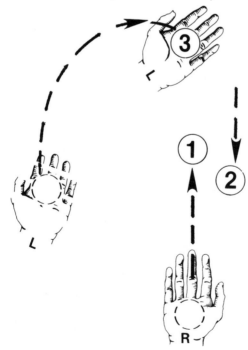

The left hand holds ball number three.

The Art of Juggling

As ball number one continues up in its flight, your left hand continues around in a circular pattern.

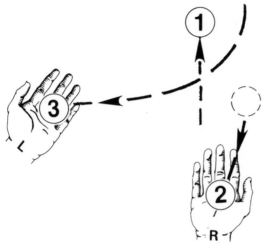

The left hand circles around each of the right hand balls.

Notice that your left hand and ball are just making a clockwise circle around one of the balls thrown from the right hand. To continue the pattern, just start making a circle each time a ball is thrown out of the right hand.

ALTERNATING UNDER BOTH LEGS

As you are juggling continuously throw a ball under your right leg, then under your left.

It is important in learning this trick that you can already go under both right and left legs separately. If you can, start by finding one odd colored juggling ball. While juggling, throw the odd colored ball under your right leg so it goes up to the left imaginary point. The odd ball will then fall to your left hand. Catch the ball with the left hand and let the hand continue down and throw the ball under your left leg and up to the right imaginary point. From there the odd ball will fall down to your right hand. Again your right hand throws it under your right leg, thus re-starting the cycle.

If you try this pattern for a while and you just can't get your legs up in the air fast enough, try warming up to the pattern by alternately throwing balls under either leg as fast as you can do the trick.

CHOPS

As you are juggling, your hands begin making large arching chops through your juggle.

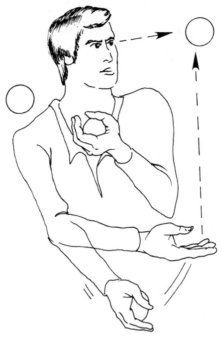

In chops, the right hand throws the ball from under the left arm.

While doing the basic cascade, wait until a ball lands in your right hand. Catch that ball and then move your right arm over to and under your left arm. From there throw the ball up, on the outside, to your left imaginary point. In other words, you are taking the right hand ball and throwing it under your left arm.

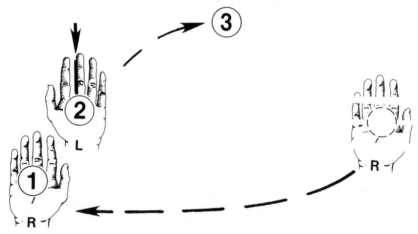

The right hand is repositioned as the left throws ball number three.

The Art of Juggling

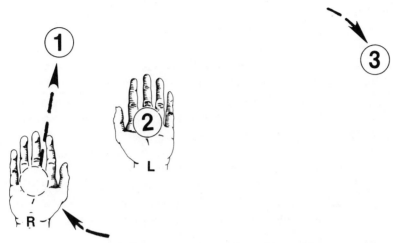

Ball number one is thrown from this position.

As ball number one continues up, bring the right hand back to its normal juggling position.

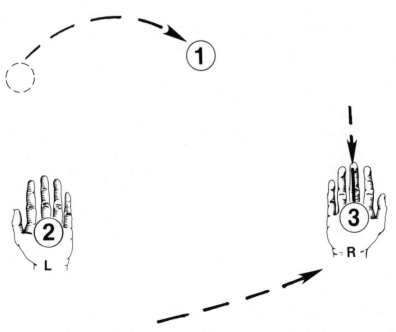

The right hand returns to position to catch number three.

Throw ball number two to the right imaginary point and then catch ball number one in your left hand. This action puts you back into the basic cascade.

Since you now understand the basic action of the chop, let me explain why this trick is called a "chop." As you try the trick you will notice that the more you practice, the more your left hand will move in an arched, rightward and down motion to let the right hand throw the ball around it. This movement of the left hand will make it seem as though you are chopping through your normal juggle.

As soon as you can do the left-hand chop, try the right-hand chop. For this you simply have your left hand throw the ball it is holding under your right hand. And, after you master the move with either hand, do every ball under your right and left hands. In other words, every throw of the balls from both hands is a "chop" movement.

BACKOFFS

As the balls are caught in either hand, your hands and arms make a fast backward motion and then a forward and down motion. This motion would be similar to the one that your arm and hand make when you are hammering a nail.

To give you an idea of the motion, take one ball and place it in your left hand. Now throw it up to the right imaginary point and then let it fall back to your right hand. As the right hand catches the ball, your hand and arm bring the ball up and back so that it can almost touch your right ear. After getting the ball there, bring it back down to your normal throwing position and throw it to your left imaginary point. As the ball falls, your left hand catches it and makes the same motion so that the ball can touch your left ear.

Once you understand the odd arm motions, you are ready to start working it into the cascade pattern. Wait until a ball is in your right hand. As soon as it gets there, make the arm motion and then throw the ball up to your left imaginary point. This move will require practice and timing because it must all be done before the next ball comes to the right hand. Keep practicing this single move until you have it down with both your right and left hands.

Then you will be ready for full backoffs. In full backoffs, every ball is brought back: right hand, left hand, right, left, and so on.

ONE OVER THE TOP

Three balls are juggled with one of the balls constantly being thrown back and forth in an arc between both hands.

Before I start the explanation of this trick it is important that you

The Art of Juggling

understand the difference in throwing a ball over or under a juggle. If you are not sure of the difference, go back and review the explanation of the reverse cascade. In this trick, the one ball going over the top is always thrown over your juggle.

With that concept in mind, start a normal cascade. As a ball almost gets to your right hand, throw the next ball over the top.

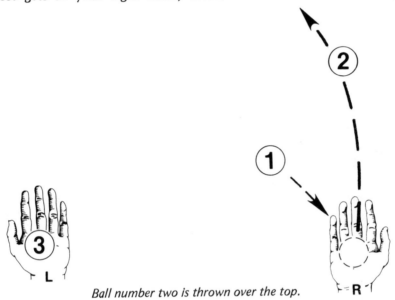

Ball number two is thrown over the top.

Let the ball go over the juggle to the far side of your left hand.

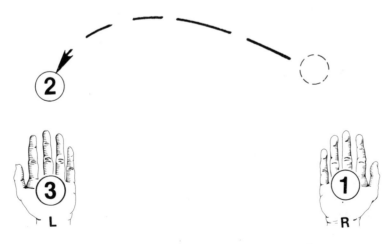

Ball number two crosses and descends to the left hand.

When the ball going over gets to your left imaginary point, throw the ball in your left hand across to your right imaginary point. When that ball gets there, throw the ball in your right hand to your left imaginary point. So, at this point you have thrown one ball over the top, then two normal throws.

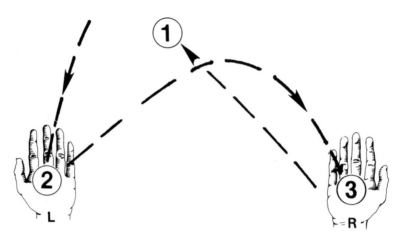

Flight pattern for one over the top.

Throw the ball in the left hand up over the ball at the left imaginary point. In other words, you will be throwing the same ball that came across the top *from* the right hand, back over the top *to* the right hand, from the left. After this you will again throw two normal throws and then the same ball will go back over the top again.

Another way of working on the trick while you are learning is to use one ball that is a different color. Get the ball to simply arc back and forth between hands, over the top of the other two balls as they continue their normal cascade pattern.

U SHAPE

All three balls are kept moving in an imaginary U pattern. The ball on your far right simply goes straight up and down on that side. The one on the left side goes straight up and down on that side. The third ball shoots straight across back and forth, between both hands.

To start the trick out of the normal cascade, throw ball number two from the right hand straight up on the outside.

The Art of Juggling

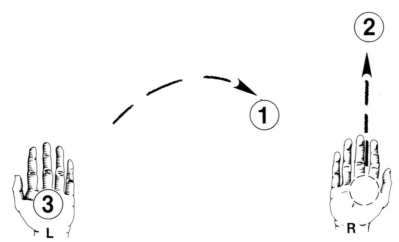

Ball number two is thrown straight up as ball number one is thrown to the right hand.

While that ball is going straight up, catch ball number one in your right hand and immediately throw it sideways straight across to your left hand. At the same time you are doing this, throw ball number three straight up to the left imaginary point.

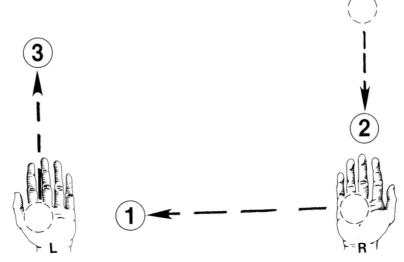

Ball number one is thrown sideways as ball number two descends and number one is thrown straight up.

As ball number one continues across, catch it in the left hand. A split second after that, catch the ball that is coming down to the right hand.

Intermediate Patterns

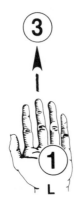

Balls one and two are caught simultaneously.

Next, throw ball number one straight across sideways toward the right hand, and at the exact same time you throw the ball in the right hand straight up to the right imaginary point.

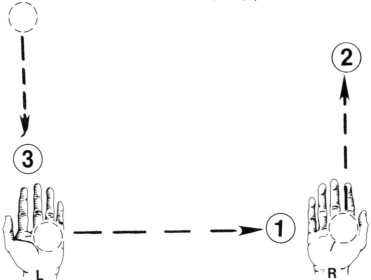

U Shape.

Your right hand catches ball number one as your left hand, right after that, catches the ball that is coming down to your left hand. After that, throw ball number one straight across sideways toward your left hand while at the same time throwing the ball in your left hand straight up to the left imaginary point. This puts you back into the cycle.

WATERFALL

The juggling balls travel in a high shower pattern. The only thing that is changed from the normal shower is the position of the left arm and hand.

Flight pattern for the waterfall.

Extend your left arm and hand up towards your left imaginary point and lock your elbow out straight. Keeping your arm in that position, do a shower pattern. Your right hand throws the balls up a few inches above your extended left hand instead of in the normal pattern; the balls never change positions vertically. Your left hand then drops the balls to your right hand instead of throwing them sideways.

ABOVE YOUR HEAD

In this trick, you are juggling in a normal cascade pattern, except the balls are up straight over your head.

The easiest way to learn this trick is to throw one ball out of a normal cascade straight up in an arc above your head. As the ball goes up, lean your head back and bring your hands back and up by your head. Now all you have to do is keep the juggle going in this position. It will help you to keep the balls in a vertical line, even with your eyes.

SNAP OUT

As you are juggling three balls in the normal cascade pattern, one ball seems to snap straight out sideways. The hand on that side seems to reach out just in time to catch the ball and pull it back into the normal juggle.

I am going to explain the trick with the ball being thrown from the right hand and going way out to the left. Once you master that, you should try throwing the ball from the left hand out to the right.

To learn, wait until a ball is in your right hand, then throw it sideways to the left. It should go directly over the top of your left hand, at a height of three to four inches. It is important when throwing

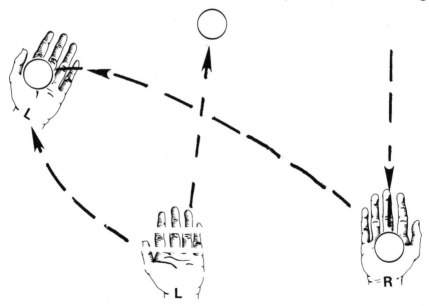

The left hand is repositioned to catch the right hand ball.

The Art of Juggling

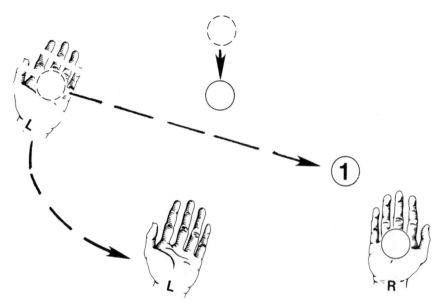

The left hand throws back the ball and returns to position.

this ball that you throw it fairly hard. As the ball passes over your left hand, which is beginning to reach sideways, that hand throws the ball it is holding straight up in the air to the right imaginary point and then the right hand immediately reaches out and catches the first ball.

As soon as your left hand catches ball number one, it throws it back, fairly hard toward the right. It should pass under the ball that is coming down from the left imaginary point.

From here, the left hand catches the ball coming down to it. The right hand waits until ball number one is a little closer and then it throws the ball it has been holding under ball number one up to the left imaginary point. Then the right hand catches ball number one. This will put you back into the normal cascade pattern.

This is not a continuous trick. However, you can keep it going by first doing it on one side, then on the other, and so on.
so on.

STUCK BEHIND YOUR BACK

For this move, you appear to place your hands behind your back and juggle.

In fact, you place one hand, your right one, way around behind your arched back so that it is all the way over to the left side of your body. Your left hand moves back, but it remains on the left side of your body, not behind you.

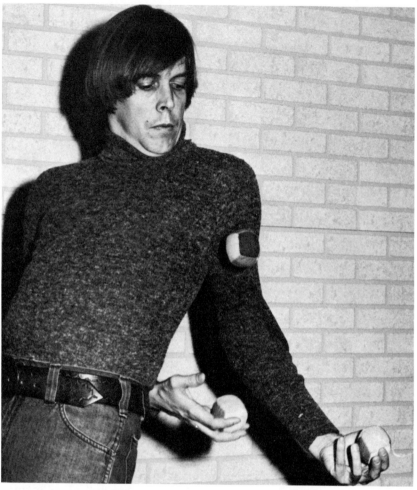

Start by juggling a cascade with your left hand behind your back.

When performing this, there are actually three tricks involved.

- You must learn to juggle in this awkward position.
- You must learn how to get from the normal cascade into this position.
- You must learn to get from this position back into a normal juggle.

To begin with step one, place two balls in your right hand and one in your left. Arch your back, and get your hands into position. Then,

The Art of Juggling

using the normal start, attempt to begin juggling. You will find that it is very difficult, but if you keep practicing, you can learn it.

Once you can keep the juggle going in this awkward position, you are ready to learn how to get there from the normal cascade. As you are juggling, throw a ball from your right hand up to a point about two feet directly above your left shoulder. When this ball drops down directly to your left side, it should (at waist level) be about a foot and a half out from your body. While the ball is doing the above, arch your back and place your right hand and arm way around behind you until your hand is over on your left side. As soon as your right hand gets in position, it throws the ball it is holding up to a point above your left hand. And, your right hand catches the first ball that it threw to the left of your body.

At this point, you should have one ball in your right hand, one in your left and one in the air above your left hand. You should be in a position that allows you to keep the behind-your-back juggle going. So, you must simply keep it going.

This brings us to the third part of the trick, getting the juggle from behind you back to a normal cascade. To accomplish this, throw a ball from your left hand up and over to your real right imaginary point. Then quickly bring your right hand back to its normal position, thus putting you back into a normal cascade pattern.

THREE IN ONE HAND

In this move, keep all three balls going using only one hand. I will explain four variations, or different patterns, for three balls in one hand. However, you should work on learning them with either hand.

This first variation is the clockwise circular pattern. This is the same as the circular two balls in one hand pattern except you have three balls. When you are first learning this there are three things to keep in mind.

● The method you use for holding the balls at the start is of great importance as you must have control of each ball individually. I find the best way is as described earlier. If you hold the balls using this method, you can throw them out individually with control.

● Never forget your imaginary point. Imagine the point a little higher than usual, but always throw the ball up to it.

● Finally, remember to keep the balls traveling in a circular pattern, not straight up and down. In other words, you have to throw them so they slide around past each other in their circular pattern.

The next, totally different three-balls-in-one-hand pattern is to keep each ball going straight up and down. This is a non-circular pattern; the balls never change positions vertically. If you go back and refer to the second variation on two balls in one hand, this is the pattern except your hand has to move faster and with more accuracy because you have one extra ball to keep up there.

The next pattern is a basic cascade done with one hand. Keep the things I mentioned about the first pattern in mind. However, instead of one point, you now have two.

The two flight patterns for three balls in one hand.

The imaginary points are from three to five feet above your right hand and approximately four inches apart.

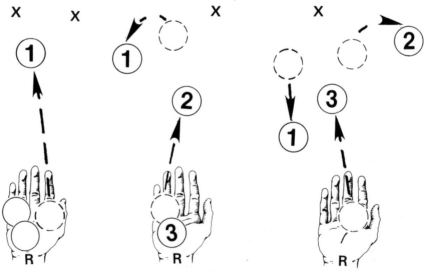

Throwing sequence for three in one hand.

The Art of Juggling

The pattern is a normal cascade done with one hand instead of two.

The fourth and final variation is one you will not see very often. Start with all three balls in your right hand. Throw the first one up and then throw the next two up together. Then catch the first one you threw up.

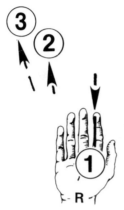

Ball number one is caught as numbers two and three are thrown up.

From here, the right hand goes around to the right and up over the lowest of the two balls in the air. Then it grabs hold of that lower ball.

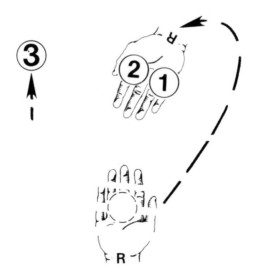

The right hand grabs the lower ball in flight.

Your right hand continues down as it turns back to the palm up position. As soon as your hand gets back to the normal throwing position, you immediately throw the two balls in your right hand back up in the air and then catch the one that is coming down. This puts you back in the position shown in the first diagram, so all you have to do is keep the cycle going. Again, this is a difficult pattern that will require a lot of practice.

OVER HEAD AND BACK

As you are juggling, throw one ball so it goes straight up over your head and then drops behind your back. As it is dropping behind your back, your left hand goes around behind your back and catches it. Then the left hand throws the ball back over the shoulder to the front so you again start juggling in a cascade pattern.

Start with just one ball in your right hand. Throw it up about a foot and a half above your head so that it will drop down behind you fairly close to your back. As you throw the ball up and over, lean your head way back and watch the ball go over. Remember, throw it straight over your head to the middle of your back, close to your body and *keep your eyes on it* as it goes over.

If you concentrate on the above while you are practicing you will soon be able to catch the ball behind your back with your left hand. Once you can catch it, practice throwing it back over the right shoulder to the front, aiming for the right imaginary point.

Once you can throw one ball back and forth, you are ready to try the move out of a three ball juggle. While doing the normal cascade, wait until a ball is in your right hand, then throw it up and back over your head. As soon as you make this throw, catch the ball that is coming down to the right hand. Then immediately place the ball that the left hand is holding into the right hand and get it back behind your back so that it can catch the ball that is dropping behind your back.

Once you catch the ball, throw it back over to the front. When your left hand throws the ball over, reach around in front and catch the same ball with the same left hand. This leaves you holding two balls in your right hand and one in your left, a perfect position for starting a normal cascade in front of you.

If you can accomplish this trick thus far, you are on the road to learning the total trick. The thing lacking is your ability to keep the two balls in the right hand moving in a two-ball-in-one-hand pattern as the left hand is behind your back. This can be accomplished by throwing the ball from your right hand up and behind your back and then catching the next ball that is coming to the right hand.

Now, instead of immediately placing the ball from the left hand over into the right hand, throw it up to the right imaginary point. This puts the two balls in a position for a two ball juggle in the right hand, and it leaves the left hand free to go behind your back and catch the ball that you have thrown there.

This brings us to the final problem in the trick, that of getting the balls back into the normal cascade pattern. Start with your left hand behind you holding one ball and your right hand juggling two balls in one hand, in front of you. Take one of the balls your right hand is juggling and throw it over to your left imaginary point. As soon as you've done this, throw the ball in your left hand up and over your right shoulder to your right imaginary point. And then immediately move your left hand around and catch the ball that is falling from the left imaginary point. This puts you in the normal cascade pattern.

All that remains to doing the trick in its ultimate form is to put the last two steps together. Throw one ball over, juggle two in your right hand, throw the ball from behind over to the front, and again start the cascade pattern.

⑥ BALANCING

Balancing is not considered to be in the mainstream of juggling but I am still including it in this book because it is a skill that most jugglers use. Balancing is the holding of an object in the state of balance, on one's forehead or chin.

HEAD BALANCING

Get a four to five foot household broom, making sure the end away from the straw is a non-sharp, rounded end. Several authors on juggling and/or circus skills have suggested that you cut the straw end off of the broom, but the extra mass of weight at the top will make the total object easier to balance.

First learn to balance the broom upright in your right hand, or left hand if you are left-handed. With your left hand, place the broom upright on the palm of your right hand. Now, let go with your left hand and keep the broom upright by moving your right hand under the object. It is important to watch the top of the stick for the slightest movement so you will be able to adjust with your hand.

When you first begin practicing this, the stick will move quite a bit. Try to keep it upright as long as possible. The more you practice, the longer you will be able to keep the broom in balance. Once you can keep it in balance, practice to keep the top of the broom as still as possible.

When you have control of balancing the broom in both of your hands you are ready to begin work on learning to balance the broom on your forehead or chin. With your right hand *holding* the broom in an upright position, tilt your head back and place the broom on your chin or forehead.

Keep your eyes on the top of the object and move your head slightly to keep it balanced.

With your right hand, make sure the broom is in a perfect upright position and then let go.

Now, just as you watched the top of the broom and moved your hand under it when you were balancing the broom in your hand, again watch the top and simply move your *head* under the broom.

At first the broom will move all over the place and your head will really have to work to keep it upright, but with practice it will become easier. Remember, though, no matter how much you practice, a broom with a rounded end will never "sit" on your head in balance. You always need to move your head to keep it in balance.

Once you become competent with broom balancing, try balancing different kinds of objects such as umbrellas, spinning plates on sticks, swords, balls on long sticks, trays of glasses on poles, tennis racquets, etc.

Or try balancing a broom on your head and juggling at the same time.

FOOT BALANCING

Another basic balancing trick is to balance a broom handle only, 2 to 2½ feet in length, on your foot.

The final *difficult* variation of the foot balance is to flip the broom handle over for one half turn with a kick of your foot and then re-catch it back in a balance, on your foot.

FEATHER AND TUBE

For this balancing sequence you will need a peacock feather of about two feet in length, plus a one-half inch tube of about two feet in length. Slide the peacock feather in the tube and hold the tube to your mouth and blow the feather up in the air.

As the peacock feather goes up in the air, it will have the quill end up. As it begins to come down the quill end will come down first. When the feather comes down, catch it in a balance upon your forehead. You will find that keeping the feather balanced is much easier than a heavier object because you have time to move under it.

Once you have the feather balanced, let it begin to fall forward, then quickly get back under it. This is one balancing trick that you can have quite a bit of fun with, and your friends will like watching it.

7 NUMBERS JUGGLING

This chapter contains the basic explanations for juggling more than three objects. The diagrams show, and the explanations are about, balls. However, the patterns are identical for any other juggling prop.

FOUR

Basic Pattern. Most people are quite surprised to learn the basic pattern with four balls is simply juggling two balls in your right hand and two balls in your left. The balls never cross to opposite hands during the juggle.

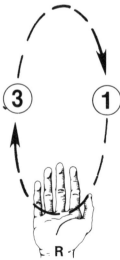

Juggling four balls is simply juggling two in each hand.

Notice that the two balls in both hands are circling from the inside of your juggle to the outside.

Your right hand is throwing its two balls in a clockwise circle that is parallel to your body, and your left hand is throwing in a counter-clockwise circle.

Another important step in learning the four ball basic juggle is establishing the *alternating* throwing pattern of each hand. Just as your hands alternate throws in a basic three ball cascade, so do they in a basic four ball juggle. In fact, the alternating tempo of throws is basically the same; right, left, right, left, etc.

As you are practicing the basic four ball juggle, be sure to keep the height of all the balls thrown the same. The actual height you throw the balls will vary according to the individual, but most beginners seem to have the most success when throwing all the balls about a foot and a half to two feet above the top of their head.

Pairs. For this four ball pattern you still juggle two balls in your right hand and two in your left. But, instead of throwing the balls in an alternating tempo, you now throw them in unison.

 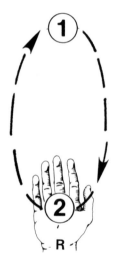

In pairs, the balls are thrown in unison.

To keep the four ball pairs pattern going, simply make every throw with your left and right hand in unison.

Shower. Every ball's pattern is a circular motion from the right hand up in the air down to the left hand, then straight across to the right.

The Art of Juggling

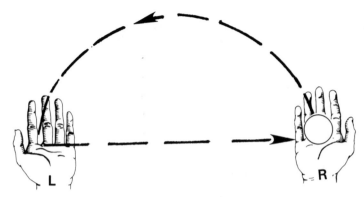

Flight pattern for the shower.

Assuming you have mastered the three ball shower, place three balls in your right hand, holding them as you would for "three balls in one hand." Place the fourth ball in your left hand. You are now ready to begin. Start by quickly throwing out all three balls in your right hand, making sure the balls are all thrown in the circular pattern.

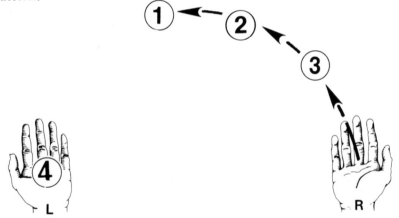

Balls one, two and three are thrown from the right hand while the left hand holds ball four.

When you get to this point, throw the ball from your left hand across to your right.

Now you are into the four ball shower so the only trick to keeping the pattern going is practice. Again, the basic rhythm or throwing pattern is similar to the three ball shower, except you make your throws a little higher and a little faster to fit the extra ball into the pattern.

Numbers Juggling

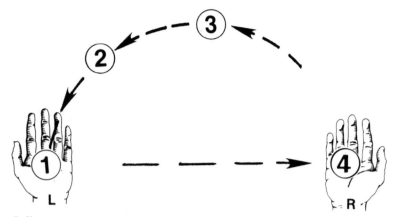

Ball number four should be caught simultaneously with ball number one.

Double Shower. Toss two balls at the same time, one from the right hand, one from the left. Both balls take semi-circular flight patterns to the opposite hand.

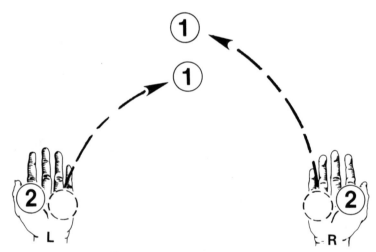

Starting the double shower.

Notice that one ball goes under the other. This is so they don't collide. Throw the next two balls in the same pattern when the first two balls reach the height of their semi-circular flight patterns, the point in time where they cross the center. You are now doing the double shower with four balls.

Cross Over. For the cross over your timing is the same as in the "double shower" except the balls cross in the center between your

The Art of Juggling

hands. There is a similarity between this and the double shower, however, in this pattern the balls take direct, not circular, flight patterns.

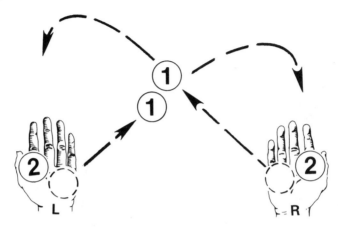

Cross over.

You have just thrown out the first two balls. Notice that the ball thrown from the left hand goes slightly under the ball thrown from the right. As these two balls reach their respective imaginary points, throw out the second two in the same pattern, and immediately catch the first two balls as they come down. This is the pattern: keep it going from this point by repeating the process.

Another way of analyzing this pattern is to think of it as simply doing four balls "in pairs" and then crossing the balls between hands on every throw.

Basic Pattern, Non Circular. This pattern is similar in timing and appearance to the basic four ball pattern, except instead of the balls in each hand making a circular motion, they will go up and down in the same vertical plane.

Non-Circular Pairs. This is the same as doing the above non-circular pattern except you throw the balls in unison.

Spread. The balls are thrown in sets of two in non-circular pattern. First, both of your hands throw one set of two balls up a little to the right of your normal juggling area. Then, both hands go over to the left side of your normal juggling area and throw up the other set of two balls.

From this point your hands must get back over to catch and then re-throw the first set of balls. From that point on, it's a matter of

Basic Pattern, Non Circular.

keeping the first and second sets of balls going *straight* up and down in their respective planes.

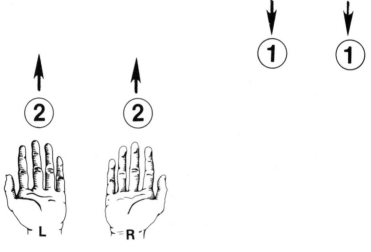

The spread pattern.

Odd Variations On Four. The basic eight patterns for doing four balls are the basics. By using your own imagination and some of the three ball patterns, you can develop many other four ball patterns. Examples are alternating under the leg throws, alternating over the shoulder throws, alternating bouncing on the head throws, etc. The possibilities with four are only as limited as your own imagination and skill.

FIVE

Learning to keep five balls in the air at one time is a real experience for the student of "numbers" juggling. Both your friends and other jugglers will begin to recognize that you are a serious student of juggling when you have mastered five. Because of the hours of practice required to learn five, once you learn it you will feel a new inner sense of accomplishment. And, after learning five you will find you have opened the door to "numbers" juggling, a field few people ever enter.

The pattern of the balls' flight for five is the same as the flight pattern for three balls, except that your imaginary points are 1½ feet higher than they are in your three ball pattern.

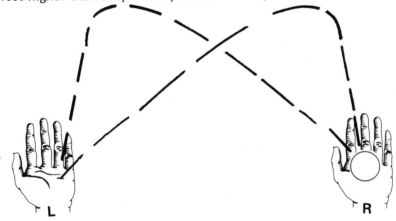

In five ball juggling, the imaginary points are 1½ feet higher than in three ball juggling.

It is important that you understand that as in a three ball cascade, balls thrown from the right hand go up to the left imaginary point and then drop down to the left hand. The balls thrown from the left hand go up to the right imaginary point and then fall to the right hand. The balls' patterns, therefore, *cross* between your hands in the air.

To start, place three balls in your right hand and two in your left. Refer back to "three balls in one hand" for the correct method of holding the three balls. As you begin trying five balls, throw the first out of your right hand cluster of three. After the first throw, alternate throws from each hand just as you do in a three ball cascade.

Hold the five balls in your hand, three in the right, two in the left. As you begin, only think about throwing the first three balls out fast and accurately to their imaginary points. This is similar to "three balls high," except you only throw the balls up about a foot and a half above your normal juggling height. It is important that the first ball is thrown from your right hand, since it contains three balls.

At this point you are ready to start five. Throw out the first three, but instead of waiting and then catching them, throw out the next two in the same alternating order.

Remember, five balls is a very difficult juggling feat and it could take hundreds of tries before you learn to keep the balls up in the air. It is best to practice where your juggling balls won't roll away. For instance, in a sandbox at an elementary school, or in the sand at the beach, or over a bed.

There are four points to remember as you are practicing. First, juggling five balls is the same basic pattern as juggling three except the balls are thrown a little higher, and your hands move ever so slightly faster. Second, make sure the balls *cross* in the center of your juggle and then continue up and sideways to their imaginary points. Third, keep all of the balls going up the same height in the air. And fourth, it is going to take practice and time to learn five.

Solidifying Your Five Juggle. Once you begin to keep your five ball pattern going, it will be similar to the first few weeks you learned to juggle three. Your pattern will probably be unsure and inaccurate.

Practice juggling five as often as you can and when you are practicing, think about keeping your hands and arms down about gut level. Try relaxing your muscles, especially your shoulder muscles.

As your pattern begins to improve, begin to work on throwing the balls up as high as you can. Then try keeping the pattern going as low as you can. Try walking forward and backward as you juggle five. Try turning in a circle. Try juggling five any chance you get.

Five Ball Tricks. All of the tricks that I am going to list here are ones that I have personally seen jugglers do with five balls. You will find that even after mastering the basic five ball pattern, tricks with five balls will be difficult. This is true with all numbers juggling; the more balls you have in the air, the harder it will be to do tricks. But, many amateur and professional jugglers do learn tricks with five balls. So, I have included the following list so you may begin work on tricks with five balls.

- under right, under left leg
- alternating under both legs

- around back
- backcrosses
- over shoulder, right or left
- over shoulders solids
- half shower
- shower
- head bounce
- knee bounce
- neck catch
- one high
- reverse cascade
- over head
- 3 in one hand, two in other
- 1 high pirouette
- 5 high pirouette

If any of these tricks are unfamiliar to you, I suggest that you refer to their descriptions in the three ball tricks section of this book. They are the same with five balls, except you have the other two balls to keep in the pattern at the same time.

MORE THAN FIVE OBJECTS

If you have mastered the juggling of five objects and are seriously thinking about learning to juggle more than five, you will need very little explanation of the technique required. For odd numbers such as seven or nine, the pattern would be the same as with three or five, except you have more balls to keep in the pattern. For six, you simply do three in each hand. Eight is done with four in each hand. In other words, for odd numbers, the objects are thrown in a cascade pattern so they cross from hand to hand. And for even numbers, you do equal amounts in both hands, in a non-crossing pattern.

How many objects can one juggler keep in the air with his two hands? I have personally seen jugglers juggle seven and eight objects at a time. I have a movie of a young Russian, Sergei Ignatov, doing nine rings at one time. And I have a still photograph of him throwing up eleven rings in a juggling pattern. These are incredible feats.

No one can say for certain what the potential is. But, I do know that anyone who can juggle even five objects has accomplished a feat that very few people ever learn.

(8) BOUNCING TRICKS

These tricks require that you use balls with a great deal of bounce. You can obtain them at most magic shops and many toy stores. Bouncing tricks are among the most interesting and enjoyable of juggling patterns.

HEAD BOUNCE

A ball is thrown up in the air and as it comes down, you bounce it off of your head, it bounces back up in the air and then you continue with your juggle.

This trick should not take too much practice if you have balls that bounce well off of your head. As you are juggling, and when a ball gets in your right hand, throw it up in the air about a foot above your head. As the ball comes down, lean your head back and let the ball hit on the flat part of your forehead.

If you aim the ball with the slant of your head, you will soon be able to bounce the ball back up toward your right imaginary point. Once you can get the ball to bounce back up to your right imaginary point, you simply throw the ball in the right hand to the left imaginary point and catch the falling ball. This will put you back into your basic cascade juggle.

Here is an extra trick that is a variation of this. Keep one small juggling ball bouncing on your forehead. You may have seen a practicing soccer player keep a large soccer ball bouncing on his forehead. This is the same trick except it is much harder to control the trick with a small ball.

When trying to learn this trick, be sure to keep your head back so your forehead is perpendicular to the up and down flight of the

The Art of Juggling

bouncing ball. This gives a flat surface for the ball to bounce on. Also, since it is easier to do with a large ball, learn it with a big soccer ball.

KNEE BOUNCE

A ball is dropped down out of a juggle and your right knee and leg bend to meet it. This action bounces the ball back up to the right imaginary point and from there you go back into the basic cascade.

The main secret to learning this trick is learning how hard and in what area around the knee the ball must bounce in order to give it a good straight bounce back up. Since everyone's legs and muscles are different, you have to work out the trick for yourself. However, for me the best place to let the ball bounce is about four inches above my knee. This point seems to be flat and yet it is far enough out on my leg so that there is enough upward motion to kick the ball up to the right imaginary point.

As you are practicing this trick, you will find it difficult to control the direction the ball will bounce off of your leg. This will come with practice.

When trying the trick from a cascade juggle it is best to learn to throw the ball that is going to bounce so you throw it out of the left hand when the ball is bouncing on the right leg.

After you learn the trick with your right leg, learn it with your left. Then try bouncing every other ball on an opposite leg. This involves bouncing a ball on the right leg, catching it in a juggle and then bouncing another ball on your left leg. Then you catch this ball in a juggle again and restart the cycle by bouncing a ball on your right leg.

Another variation of the knee bounce is to keep one ball bouncing back and forth between both legs, without the use of your hands. This requires a lot of practice, and I would suggest that you first learn the trick with a larger ball, before attempting it with a smaller juggling ball.

FOOT BOUNCE

From a juggle, drop a ball down in front of you, and, just before the ball hits the ground, kick it back up into a juggle with your foot.

The best way to learn this trick is to throw a ball up in the air as you did in one ball high. Then as the ball comes down, let it bounce on the ground. After it bounces and starts to come up, this is the point at which you give it a little kick. Actually you are merely push-

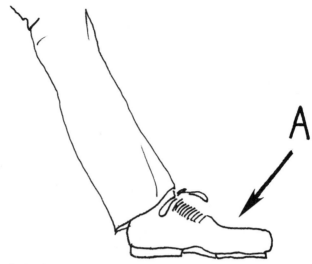

The ball should bounce off the top of the foot, not the toes.

ing the ball up, not really kicking it. It is best to wear hard shoes that have a more or less flat surface over the toe area.

Notice you are not kicking the ball with the end of your toes, but more with the top of your foot. And it is important to keep this part of your shoe flat when you are kicking the ball so that it will bounce straight up.

After you can kick the ball up from a bounce, learn it without the bounce. In other words, throw a ball from the right hand out in front of you and before it hits the ground, kick it back up to your right imaginary point. Then, all you have to do is go back into your cascade juggle.

KNEE FOOT BOUNCE

A ball leaves a normal cascade juggle to bounce first on your right knee, then as the ball is about to hit the ground, it is kicked by the right foot back into the normal cascade pattern.

Both of the individual parts of this trick, knee bounce and foot bounce, were just described. However, when these two tricks are placed together, they form a new and more difficult trick.

To start, throw a ball out from the right hand so that it goes in front of and above your right knee. When the knee comes up to meet the ball, do not bring it up as far as you did when trying to knee bounce the ball back into a normal cascade pattern. Instead, bounce the ball off your knee so that it goes a few inches out in front of your knee and then drops toward the ground. In other words, bounce the ball off of your knee so that it is in a good position to be kicked back up by your right foot.

Once the ball gets down above your right foot, your foot comes up and kicks the ball back up to your right imaginary point. Once the ball gets back to your right imaginary point, simply let it drop back down into your normal cascade juggle.

ARM BOUNCE

While you are juggling, throw a ball from your right hand over to your left arm. The ball bounces off of your left arm and you go right back into the juggle.

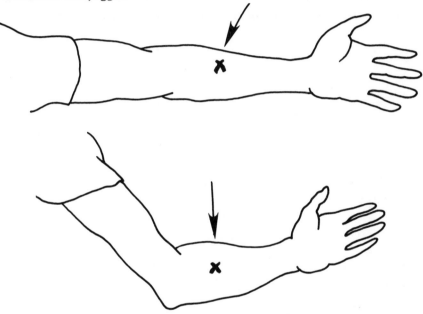

If you place your left arm out in the above position with your palm up, X marks the spot where the ball should bounce. Hold one ball in your right hand and then throw it across to point X on your left arm. With your left arm, bat the ball back up and over to your right imaginary point. Then as the ball descends, catch it in your right hand.

When you are able to control this trick by bouncing one ball off of the left arm, try the trick from a three ball juggle. When a ball gets into your right hand, throw it over to the left arm and bat it back to the right imaginary point, and then start juggling again. While the one ball is bounced off of your arm, the other two balls are held one in each hand.

There are two variations of the arm bounce that I will mention here:

● Hold two balls in your right hand and one in your left. Every time a ball is thrown from your right hand, it bounces off of the left arm back toward the right hand. This is the same as juggling two balls in your right hand except that each ball is bouncing off of your left arm.

● For this variation, you must learn to bounce a ball off of your right arm as well as your left. This variation is known as alternating arm bounces.

To start this variation, throw a ball from your right hand over to your left arm where it bounces up to your right imaginary point.

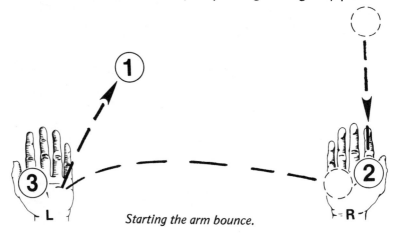

Starting the arm bounce.

When that ball hits there, throw the ball in your right hand to the left imaginary point.

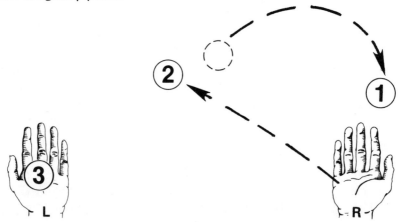

Ball two is thrown to the left imaginary point as ball one descends.

The Art of Juggling

When this ball gets there, throw the ball that your left hand has been holding over to your right arm. At this point you are half-way through the cycle.

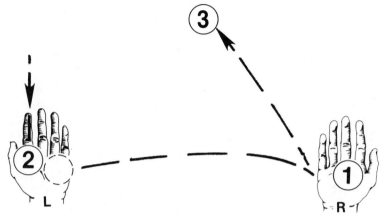

The halfway point in the arm bounce.

When the ball gets to your right arm, bounce it up to the left imaginary point.

Then, when that ball gets there throw the extra ball to your right imaginary point.

When this ball gets to your right imaginary point, throw the right hand ball to your left arm, thus restarting the cycle.

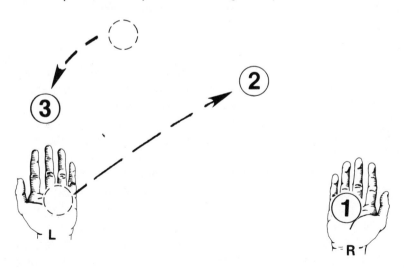

Ball number two is thrown to the right imaginary point, restarting the cycle.

SNAP ARM BOUNCE

As you are juggling, throw a ball from your left hand over toward your right arm just as in the previous trick. However, in this trick instead of batting the ball with your arm, you snap it with a fast extension of your right arm.

Once you can do this trick with your right arm, then learn it with your left. Also work on learning all of the variations in this chapter, with the snap instead of bounce.

Another variation is the one ball on one arm bounce. Most professional ball jugglers will use this in a juggling routine after they have done some of the variations of the arm bounce or snap arm bounce. The effect is one ball bouncing up and down for ten to fifteen bounces on your extended (palm up) arm. The controlled motion to keep the ball there is an arm movement between the batting arm and the snap arm bounce. In this move, the ball bounces only a few inches above the arm, but it must be under full control.

One final move that I will mention is an arm catch. All you do is throw a ball from the left hand over to the right arm just as if you were going to snap it. However, instead of extending your arm and batting the ball, you fold your arm so your hand and forearm come in and up toward your shoulder. Thus you are catching or trapping the ball between your upper and lower arm.

To get the ball back into the juggle, you snap your arm straight out, thus catapulting the ball up toward the left imaginary point. This puts you back into the normal cascade pattern.

CASCADE FLOOR BOUNCE

Juggle three balls by bouncing them on the floor. This trick is actually a reverse cascade done downward instead of up in the air. You have to picture two imaginary points on the floor, about ten inches apart and about two inches in front of your toes.

Since this is a reverse cascade, when a ball is thrown from the right hand, throw it downward toward the right, *not* left, imaginary point. This ball will then hit the right imaginary point and bounce up between your hands, whereupon your left hand catches it.

The opposite is true of a ball thrown from the left hand. It goes to the left point, bounces up between your hands, whereupon your right hand catches it.

Notice that the hands are turned horizontally so that your palms are facing in. This is the proper hand position for accomplishing this trick.

The Art of Juggling

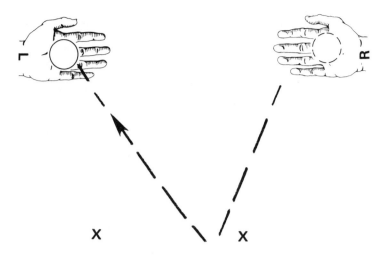

The right hand ball is thrown to the right imaginary point on the floor.

Now that you mentally understand the desired flight pattern of the balls, you have to learn timing. The floor bounce is a slower rhythm than a cascade juggle because you do not throw the second ball when the first one hits its imaginary point, but rather wait until the ball is on its way up.

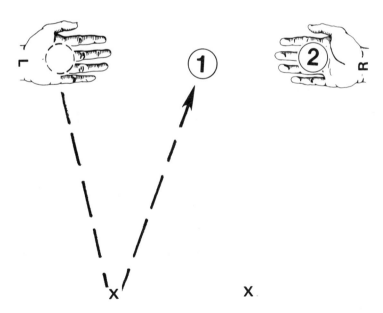

The second ball isn't thrown until the first is on its way up.

When the right hand catches ball number one, it must not wait for the ball to fall into that hand. You have to reach and grab the ball with your right hand, palm sideways.

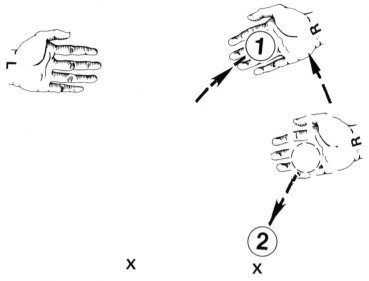

The right hand moves up to catch ball number one.

When ball number two gets to the point that it is at in the above drawing, you are ready to throw out ball number three and then catch number two.

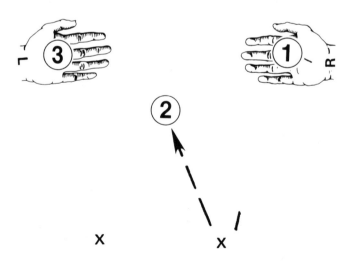

Ball number three should be held until number two is on its upward flight.

Notice that you are back to your original throw of one ball out of your left hand. To keep the trick going, just keep the cycle going. But remember the rhythm of this trick is slower than the normal cascade so do not rush the trick.

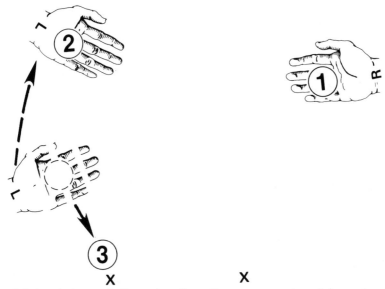

The left hand throws ball number three then moves up to catch number two.

SHOWER FLOOR ROLL

This trick is not a bouncing trick but it fits in a routine nicely after you do the cascade floor bounce. Instead of trying to describe the appearance of the trick to you, I am going to explain the pattern for one ball.

With one ball in your right hand place both of your hands on the ground about two inches in front of your feet. You will need to squat down to do this. It is important that your palms are up. Next, turn your hands inward toward each other so your fingertips are pointing toward each other. With your hands in this position, move them away from each other until your fingertips are about fourteen inches apart.

Now let the one ball you are holding in your right hand roll out onto the floor toward the left hand. The left hand picks the ball up and throws it in a slight arc in the air back over to the right hand.

That is one ball going once around. Next try keeping one ball going round and round. Then try it with two balls. And once you are getting it with two you are ready to try it with three.

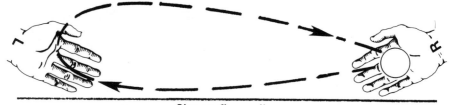

Shower floor roll.

Start with two balls in your right hand and one in your left. Roll out the two balls from the right hand and then throw the one from the left across. This will set the pattern up, all you have to do is keep it going.

Keep the following in mind while you are trying the trick:

● You must throw all of the balls from the left hand high enough so that they do not hit the balls rolling from the right.

● The tempo the balls roll across you control. So work to make each ball roll slowly and at the same pace!

SHOWER FLOOR BOUNCE

This is another form of floor bounce juggling, however in this method you bounce the balls in a shower formation.

To learn the trick, visualize one spot on the floor. This spot should be between your feet and in front of them about two inches. The flight pattern will be from your right hand down to that point on the floor, up to the left hand, from the left hand straight across sideways to your right hand. This is the same as the three ball shower except your hands throw the balls down instead of up.

Start with two balls in your right hand and one in your left. Throw out the two in your right hand and then throw the one from your left straight across to your right hand. This will set up the pattern and all you have to do is keep it going.

CASCADE BOUNCE WITH ONE UNDER LEG

While juggling in a cascade, floor bounce style, raise your right leg so that one of the bouncing balls goes under it.

I am going to describe the trick using the right leg. After you have mastered it with the right leg, you should learn it with your left leg also.

Start by having one ball in your right hand. As you start to throw the ball down to your right imaginary floor point, raise your right leg up and begin to move it slightly over to your right. The rightward

The Art of Juggling

motion of the leg has to be coordinated with the bounce of the ball. When the ball actually bounces on the floor, your right leg should be up in the air and directly over the ball but still continuing to the right. As the ball starts its path back up from the floor your leg comes back down to the floor. That is the basic timing. So, to do the trick from the three ball floor bounce, just raise your leg as you throw a ball from your right hand.

For throwing under your left leg, the timing is the same. You just do everything opposite. And after you have mastered the trick under either leg, try keeping it going by alternating throws under both legs.

⑨ PARTNERS JUGGLING

Partners juggling is the throwing of juggling props between two or more jugglers, and may be broken down into three main categories:

- two people passing
- side by side passing
- group formation passing.

Two people passing is the systematic throwing of props between two jugglers facing each other, or two jugglers standing back to back.

On the other hand, side by side passing is, as its name implies, the throwing of props between two jugglers who are standing side by side.

And finally, group formation passing is the passing of props between three or more jugglers. In group formation passing there is the possibility of combining face to face, back to back, face to back, and side by side juggling patterns.

I am going to explain the basic patterns with all three groups using balls. However, it is my personal belief that the real heart of partners juggling is in the passing of objects bigger and more obvious than balls. Therefore, I would encourage you to work on passing rings, clubs, or club-like objects as soon as possible.

Every juggler involved in partners passing patterns must have control of his basic cascade. And, everyone involved must have the ability to "look through" his juggling pattern in order to see his juggling partner.

Everyone involved must, in partners, be juggling at the same tempo. So, before you begin it would be good for everyone to simply stand around and try juggling in-tempo with everyone else.

If you have control of your basic juggle, and you are all juggling at the same tempo, you are ready to begin work on partners juggling.

TWO PEOPLE PASSING

Basic Passing Pattern. To begin your work in two people passing, you and your partner should stand facing each other somewhere between six and twelve feet apart. As you begin getting into two people passing you will be able to determine the most comfortable distance. Next, make sure your feet are planted firmly on the ground with your left foot forward from your right by about a foot.

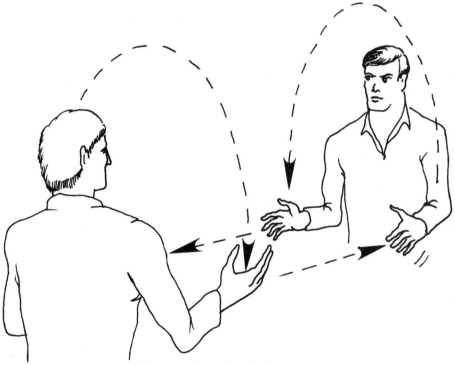

Two people passing, basic pattern.

To begin, just try throwing one or two balls around in the above pattern. As you are doing so note that there are two different ways that balls can be thrown and caught.

The first is the most natural, but also the most inaccurate. Throw the ball from one person's right hand, up in an arc so that it drops into the other person's left hand.

The other method is for the first juggler to throw the ball with the motion of underhand pitching of a soft ball. In this case, the ball's flight pattern is much more direct and accurate. And, because of this accuracy, I would encourage you to learn this method.

If you and your partner try this throwing method it brings up another immediate problem for the juggler catching the ball: How do you get a grip on the ball to catch it? The solution is quite easy, but it will take some practice before it becomes natural. Instead of catching the ball with your palm up, put your receiving hand in the following position.

Position of receiving hand.

With your hand in this position your partner's straight throw will be easier to catch. Now, to put the ball into a normal juggling pattern, swing your hand in a counter clockwise, downward circle. As your hand goes down below waist level and then begins back up, let go of the ball into a normal juggling pattern, throwing the ball to your right imaginary point.

Your next step toward two people passing is learning to start together. For passing there are two sequences to which I am referring. First, both jugglers must begin by throwing their first ball into their own juggling pattern at the same time. Secondly, both jugglers must throw the balls to be exchanged at the same time.

There is a "standard" starting procedure that many jugglers have used. For passing six balls between two people, each juggler starts with two balls in his right hand and one in his left. Now, both jugglers raise their right hands above their heads. At this point, when both people have their hands in the air, the leader lowers his right hand at a normal juggling speed. As the hand drops a little below waist level, it begins moving upward and releases the first ball across to his left imaginary point. In other words, after both jugglers signify they are ready by raising their right hands, the leader begins juggling to himself with a deliberate lowering of his right hand. As the leader is doing this, the other partner lowers his right hand and starts his juggle to himself at exactly the same time, in tempo with the leader. If this exercise is successful, both jugglers should be starting together, in tempo.

The next question is which ball is first thrown to the other juggler. Let's go back to the point where both have their right hands raised. Notice the ball in your left hand. This is the ball that you will throw to your partner.

First, throw one ball from your right hand to your left imaginary point. Next, throw the ball in your left hand to your right imaginary point. Then throw the second right hand ball to your left hand point. Now, at this point you are ready to take the left hand ball, which has been caught in your right hand, and in tempo with your normal juggling speed and pattern throw it across to your partner.

Your throw should be made so that your ball goes directly to the top of your partner's left shoulder. If your throw has been placed properly, in tempo, your partner should now be able to catch the ball and still continue in tempo, lowering his left hand and throwing the ball into his own juggling pattern.

It is important you understand the process by which your partner puts his hand up, catches the ball you have thrown, lowers his hand, and throws the ball into his own juggling pattern, because, if your partner started at the same time you did and threw his ball toward you at the same time you threw yours toward him, you will have to catch the ball he has thrown. Catch it with your left hand, lower your left hand and throw the ball into your normal juggling pattern, via your right imaginary point.

If you and your partner can do the above exercise correctly, not only will you have passed and caught two balls between you, but you will also both still be juggling in tempo with each other. If you haven't done it right, keep practicing until you can. After you can start together, throw the first set of balls across to each other, catch the balls, throw them into your own juggle, and both continue juggling in-tempo, you are ready to go on.

Start by attempting to throw every third ball across to each other. Begin as you did before, with the first left hand ball across. But this time, as you catch the ball from your partner, keep your eyes on it as you continue your own juggle. When this ball gets to your right hand, instead of throwing it to your left imaginary point, again throw it to your partner. Catch the one your partner throws and watch it until it gets to your right hand. Then throw it to your partner. If you keep this sequence going in a nice even tempo you are now passing "thirds." Another way of analyzing this throwing pattern is that your right hand throws every third ball to your partner. Your right hand throws two balls, one at a time, into your normal juggling pattern, one to your partner, two into your normal pattern, one to your partner, etc.

If you can keep every third throw to your partner going, try throwing every other right hand throw to your partner. Remember, don't rush things, keep the same tempo as if you were juggling to yourself.

Next, after a normal start, try throwing every right hand throw to your partner. This will be more difficult, so keep the following things in mind:

- Keep a normal juggling tempo.
- Keep in tempo with your partner.
- Make sure your throws to your partner are placed with accuracy, where he can catch them.
- Keep the balls you are throwing from left to right in a normal juggling flight pattern. *Don't* pass them between hands.
- Work toward passing a certain number of "solid" throws to your partner. Try three or five, and then continue on with your normal juggling pattern. This should help you and your partner to get the feel of passing "solids" or every one without developing any bad timing habits.

Three-Three-Ten. This is a two people passing sequence that appears to get faster and faster to someone who is watching.

I will analyze this juggling sequence for you from the standpoint of one partner's right hand throws. The throws are done as follows:

self-self-partner
self-self-partner
self-self-partner   3 "thirds"
self-partner
self-partner   3 "every other"
self-partner
partner
partner
partner
partner
partner   10 "solids"
partner
partner
partner
partner
partner

Bounce Passing. In this passing pattern, instead of throwing the balls directly to your partner's left hand, bounce them half-way between the two of you, so they bounce up to your partner's left hand.

Back to Back. Back to back passing is done with the same timing as face to face except the objects being passed must be thrown up and back over the right shoulder.

Back to back passing.

Three In Two Hands. You and your partner stand facing each other, as three balls are passed in a normal cascade pattern between your right hand and your partner's left. Once you can keep this going with three balls between two hands, you are ready to try six balls. Six balls is simply two separate sets of three balls in two hands. Three balls are juggled between your right and your partners left hands. And, three more balls are juggled between your left and your partner's right hand.

Reverse Direction. At the beginning of this chapter, I showed you the basic passing pattern with the objects being thrown from the right hand and caught with the left. However, another basic passing pattern that will be of great advantage in advanced group passing is two people throwing the objects with the left hand and catching them with the right. Once you and your partner have mastered one throw in the opposite pattern, then learn "thirds," "every other," "solids" and the "3, 3, 10" with the left hand.

Three Back and Forth. This effect always looks good when placed in a routine *before* you and your partner pass six objects. All you do is pass three objects *solid.* As you are starting, your right throws self, self, partner, partner, partner, pause, catch left, catch left, catch left, partner, partner, partner, pause, catch left, catch left, catch left, etc.

In other words, you throw with your right hand only, the objects to your partner. Your partner in turn throws only with his right hand after receiving them from you.

The most important element in keeping this pattern going is that you *never* "pass" an object between your left and right hand, you must always throw it into your normal juggling pattern.

Three Objects—Both Hands—Back and Forth. Throw three objects from both of your hands, to your partner. If you are doing a normal cascade, wait until you are ready to throw a normal right hand toss to your partner's left hand. Then throw the ball that is in *your* left hand to your partner's right hand.

As soon as you've thrown that ball, throw the last ball from your right hand to your partner's left hand.

Having caught the objects, your partner will then begin throwing them back to you in exactly the same manner. Two things will help you on this pattern. First, practice "reverse" passing mentioned earlier in this chapter. And second, just keep trying it.

Once you have mastered this, do the same pattern and tempo but cross the throws. Your right hand throws will be going to your partner's right hand, and your left hand throws to your partner's left hand.

Balance In-Between. While passing, the two jugglers balance an object between each other.

This trick is easiest if only one partner balances the object, while the other remains stationary.

Seven Object Passing. The passing of more than six objects is still accomplished with the objects making basically the same flight pattern as in the basic passing pattern. However, there are two differences.

• The flight pattern of the objects is an arc, instead of direct and straight across.

• In six object "solids" passing, both jugglers throw and catch each object in tempo together. However, in seven object passing, the partners must throw opposite each other, the same as your hands throw opposite each other in a basic three ball cascade.

To learn the passing of seven objects, the leader starts with four objects, two in right and two in left, and his partner starts with three objects, two in right and one in left. Both partners raise their right hands, then the leader lowers his right hand. The follower lowers his hand and begins once the leader's starting hand has reached the bottom of its initial downward movement.

From these starting points, both partners throw "solids" to each other. Watch your throws to your partner, making sure the object is coming in where he can catch it. And make sure your throws, as well as your partner's throws, are both arcing about the same height in the air.

The person starting with four balls may wonder in what order he throws them out. Start by throwing one of the right hand balls directly to your partner. Next, throw one of the left hand balls to your right imaginary point. Then, throw the second ball from the right hand directly to your partner. From this point on, your pattern is the same as if you were doing "solids" with six objects.

Finally, if you are attempting seven object passing with clubs, learn the trick using double turns with the clubs. But, after mastering it with double turns, it's challenging to try it with triple or single turns.

Eight Object Passing. For this type of passing, you and your partner throw and catch in unison, as in six object passing. To begin, each partner has four balls, two in right and two in left. In unison, both partners begin throwing the balls to each other in a high arching pattern. The objects must be thrown with speed and accuracy. I would recommend also before starting work on eight object passing that both partners can perform as "the leader" in seven object passing.

Finally, if you are using clubs, the pattern can be learned with either double or triple turns.

Throwing and Catching a Club in Passing Patterns. A club is held, thrown, and caught differently than a ball. Therefore, I have included some extra thoughts on the holding of a club for passing.

First, a club is thrown with an arm and body movement, not just a wrist movement.

Sequence for throwing and catching a club.

Notice that the hand is near the knob of the club.

As you go from this position to letting go of the club so that it can travel to your partner, your arm and body make an underhand pitching movement with the club.

From this point, the club makes a single turn right into your partners hand.

Notice three things:

- The club travels in a direct horizontal line between partners.

- The club turns end over end *once.*

- When the club reaches your partners hand, the belly is up and the knob is down.

Look closely at the hand position of the person catching the club. To get the club from this position back into the normal juggling pattern, the left hand swings the club in a counter clockwise circle down below waist level, then continuing up, it throws the club into a normal pattern.

SIDE BY SIDE PASSING

Side By Side Pattern Number One. In this first side by side pattern, each partner simply does one hand of a normal cascading pattern.

The juggler on stage left only uses his left hand while the juggler on stage right only uses his right hand.

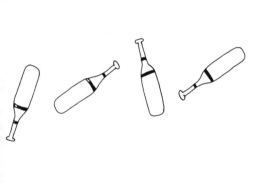

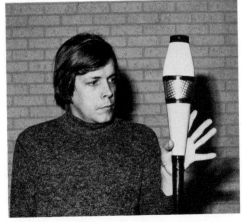

Receive the club between your thumb and forefinger, with the belly up and knob down.

Take-a-ways. The effect of this pattern is that one person is juggling three objects when a second juggler enters and takes over the juggling of the objects, with no break in the flight pattern of the objects being juggled.

The first step is for juggler number two to approach juggler number one from behind left. From this position, juggler number two puts his right hand and arm across so that it is above and behind juggler number one's right arm.

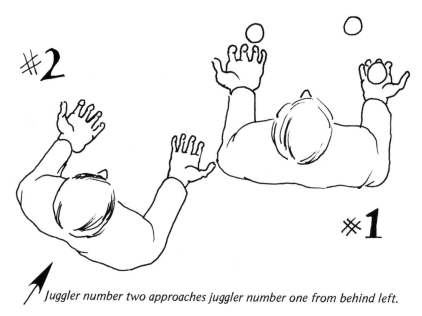

Juggler number two approaches juggler number one from behind left.

This is the one step most beginning students of "take-a-ways" don't do. If you don't put your right arm and hand across *before* taking the first ball with your *left* hand, the pattern will be rushed and very jerky, if it is completed at all.

At this point, juggler number two's left hand then catches the ball

Juggler number two reaches across to catch the ball coming to juggler number one's left hand.

The Art of Juggling

that is coming down to juggler number one's left hand. Then immediately juggler number two, with his right hand, catches the ball coming down to juggler number one's right hand. At this point, if juggler number one has continued to throw all of his tosses in his normal pattern, juggler number two should have one ball in each of his hands, and there should be one more ball going up, between his hands, to his left imaginary point.

From this stage, number two completes his forward motion and juggler number one takes a slight backward motion.

Continuous Take-A-Ways. For this move, both partners must be able to do both positions of a normal take-a-way, which involves one juggler stepping in and taking the juggle from the other.

Continuing on, juggler number one steps behind and around juggler number two and then he takes the juggle back away. Number two, stepping behind and around number one takes the juggle away from number one again. If you both keep this move going, you are doing continuous take-a-ways. And, the faster each juggler can get around and take the juggle, the better the move looks.

You can really get a comic effect from this move if it looks like the juggler who is juggling doesn't know that the second juggler is going to take the objects being juggled.

Take-A-Ways, With A Hat. This is a nice extra bit that can enhance the ending of a take-a-way sequence. During a series of take-a-ways, one juggler is wearing a funny hat. After several fast continuous take-a-ways, the jugglers begin taking the hat from each other's heads.

To accomplish the taking of the hat, wait until the juggler wearing the hat has just taken the objects from juggler number two. As juggler number two steps around behind juggler number one, his right hand takes the hat and places it on his own head. Then he continues with the normal take-a-way. You will find that with practice, this grabbing of the hat will not alter your timing of continuous take-a-ways.

Taking An Object Out. Juggler number two walks up behind juggler number one, who is juggling three balls, and takes one of the balls, leaving juggler number one juggling two balls.

There are two separate moves involved in this trick. The first is in taking one ball out of the juggle. To do this, juggler number two approaches juggler number one as in take-a-ways, then with his right hand he reaches up and takes a ball out of juggler number one's juggle.

Partners Juggling

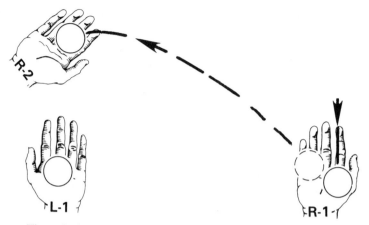

The right hand reaches up to take a ball from the other person's juggle.

The second part of the trick requires juggler number one to juggle the two balls with two hands. This is often referred to as idling. Actually, it is a very basic move in which you just keep throwing the two balls in a normal cascade pattern. Right, left, left, right, right, left, left, right, etc.

Passing Odd Objects In. As juggler number one juggles, juggler number two approaches from behind with an odd object (rubber chicken, toilet plunger, etc.), then, with his right hand, he reaches up and takes one of juggler number one's three objects. Juggler number one continues throwing the ball in his left hand to the right imaginary point, then the ball in his right hand to his left imaginary point.

Juggler number two throws the odd object he has been holding in his left hand in between juggler number one's hands and arms, to juggler number one's right imaginary point. Then juggler number one simply continues to juggle his original two objects plus the one odd object.

One Back And Forth. Partner number one is throwing one object back and forth through juggler number two's two ball idling juggling pattern.

Juggler number two holds his hands out, one ball in each hand, at about normal juggling height. Then juggler number one, standing behind and slightly to the left of juggler number two, with a ball in his left hand, reaches around to the left of juggler number two. He throws the ball his left hand is holding under and in between juggler number two's outstretched hand, up toward juggler number two's right imaginary point.

The Art of Juggling

One back and forth.

As soon as juggler number one throws the ball, he quickly moves his right hand over to the right hand side of juggler number two and catches the same ball he threw. As all of this is happening, juggler number two throws his right hand ball, then his left in a normal cascade. This is the basic two ball exchange that was the preliminary step to learning how to juggle three balls.

After the above, juggler number one throws the ball in his right hand up, through, and between juggler number two's hands, to juggler number two's left imaginary point. Juggler number two does a two ball exchange, throwing right, then left. That is the basic pattern.

Under Leg Take-A-Ways. Juggler number one stands with his legs spread apart. Juggler number two crawls under the through them and begins to stand up slowly, taking-a-way the juggle from number one.

Side By Side Passing Of More Than Three. This pattern can easily enable two jugglers to juggle five or seven objects.

With your finger, follow the balls' flight pattern. As your finger follows the balls' flight, you will find juggler number two must exchange the balls from his left to right hand as in a normal three ball shower.

However, juggler number one must exchange right to left as in a *reverse* shower. Before beginning work on this pattern, make sure

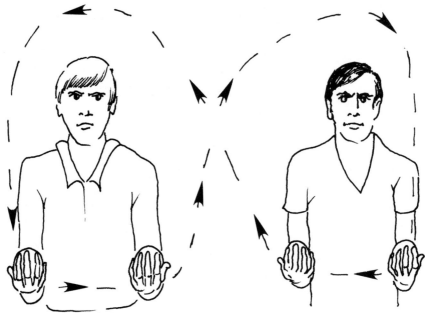

Side by side passing of more than three objects.

juggler number one can do a controlled reverse shower, and juggler number two can do a controlled three ball shower.

Once you are ready to start working on the five ball pattern, juggler number one starts with two balls in his left hand, one in his right. Juggler number two starts with one ball in each hand.

First, from juggler number one's standpoint, you throw one ball out of your left hand. Next you see juggler number two's first ball cross over to your side. At that point you throw your second left hand ball and then immediately throw the ball from your right hand straight across sideways to your left hand. You catch the first falling ball that your partner threw, in your right hand. You see your partner's next ball cross over to your side of the juggle. Then restart the cycle: throw left, throw right sideways, catch right.

Juggler number two's view and execution of the trick is as follows. After juggler number one throws his first ball over to your side of the juggling pattern, throw your right hand ball to your partner's side, in the pattern outlined earlier. As soon as you throw that ball, throw your left-hand ball straight across to your right hand. Catch the ball coming down to your left hand. At this point, you are back to the beginning of the cycle, so just keep it going with your partner.

If you watch the crossing of the balls in the center, the tempo and pattern is the same as a three ball cascade. Both jugglers must

The Art of Juggling

make their throws to their partners accurate, so their partner can catch them with the correct hand.

Once you have mastered the pattern with five balls, try seven. To start, juggler number one has two balls in his left hand and two in his right. Juggler number two starts with two balls in his right hand and one in his left.

GROUP FORMATION PASSING

Six Objects Pass-Person In Middle. Two jugglers pass six objects in a standard pattern with one non-juggling individual standing in the middle.

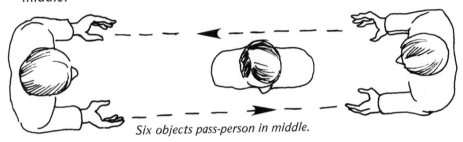

Six objects pass-person in middle.

Obviously this trick seems much more spectacular when done with clubs as compared to balls.

Six Object Pass-Person Walking Through. As two jugglers pass objects in "thirds" tempo, a third individual walks through the path of the flying objects.

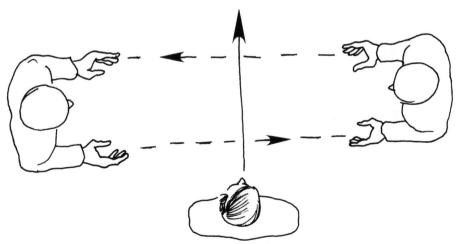

Six object passing-person walking through.

The trick to this pattern is for the individual walking through to understand the "thirds" throwing pattern so he walks through immediately after one pass, and he gets through the pattern before the next pass.

This same trick can be accomplished with an "every other" throwing tempo. Usually, immediately after the first pass, the person walking through walks into the middle of the juggle. This is the same position he would be in for six objects pass-person in middle. He then waits for the second pass and then completes his walk through.

Six Object Pass With Take-A-Ways. As two jugglers are passing objects with a solid tempo, a third juggler enters and positions himself to the left of, and next to one of the passing jugglers. He then begins receiving the objects being passed until he has replaced the juggler he is standing next to.

Although I have titled this trick "take-a-ways," the incoming juggler does not take the objects away as in take-a-ways. Instead the leader (A in drawing) begins feeding the objects to the incoming juggler's left hand.

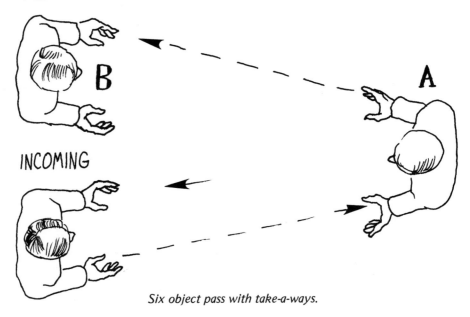

Six object pass with take-a-ways.

An important point in accomplishing this pattern is that both the incoming juggler and B keep a normal cascade pattern and tempo going as they are getting or receiving all of the objects.

I have described this trick with six objects. However, I have seen

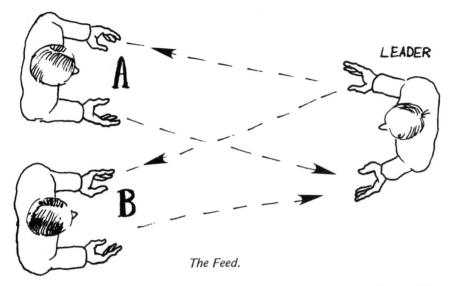

LEADER

The Feed.

it done with seven objects also. And, I would assume it is possible with eight object passing.

The Feed. This pattern gives the appearance that one juggler is passing objects with two jugglers at the same time.

In effect, the leader is first throwing and receiving one object from B, then one from A, then one from B, etc.

To begin, the leader throws every other throw, alternating between A and B. This means that both A and B are only throwing every fourth right hand throw to the leader. To get the whole thing started, all members of the group raise their right hands. Then as the leader starts, A and B also start in tempo. As the juggling proceeds, both B and the leader do a normal passing start, the third object out of the right hand being passed.

From that point on, B passes every fourth object thrown by his right hand to the leader, the rest being thrown to his own left imaginary point. The leader in turn, throws every other throw, alternating between A and B's left hands.

A, on the other hand, throws his first four right-hand throws to himself, then the fifth right hand throw is passed to the leader. And from that point on, every fourth right hand throw is passed to the leader.

You have just learned the timing for an every other feed. However, the ultimate goal in timing for the right handed feed is to have the leader passing solids, every object being alternated between A and B. To accomplish this, both A and B will be passing every others.

To start, all three jugglers begin at the same time, with both leader and B passing their first objects from a normal passing start. From this point on, B passes every other pass and the leader passes solids between B and A.

A's first object to be passed is the fourth throw out of his right hand. And from that point on, A passes every others with the leader.

All of the jugglers involved in this group passing pattern, or any group passing pattern, should really watch the accuracy and timing of their individual throws to each other. And, specifically in the feed, both A and B must work extra hard on their accuracy of throws so they help the leader out.

And finally, I have described the feed with a leader and two receivers. However, it is possible to do the trick, with different timing, with more than two receivers.

Two High Feed. For those of you who are involved in acrobatics and gymnastics, you can also try a two high feed. A word of caution: make sure you know what you are doing on a two high pyramid before attempting this trick, because B must take his hands away from A's calves in order to juggle, and this makes the two high pyramid much less stable. Therefore, it is important that all members know what to do if the whole thing collapses. Also, when first trying juggling in a pyramid, even though both A and B can do a pyramid without juggling, you will probably fall. So, make sure your first trys are in an open area so you don't fall on other people, chairs, sprinkler heads, or props.

The Triangle. Three jugglers stand in a triangle pattern and pass objects in thirds, every others, or solids tempo.

When first attempting this trick, everyone must watch the accuracy of their throws. Also only begin by trying one pass then try thirds, and slowly work your way up to a 3, 3, 10.

The Box. Four jugglers stand in a squared off pattern, passing clubs through the center of the square.

A and B are passing with each other, and C and D are passing with each other. Obviously, the object with this pattern is to work out the timing of the throws so that two clubs never get to the center crossing point at the same time.

To start, we will learn the pattern with both sets of jugglers throwing every other tempo. With all of the jugglers beginning at the same

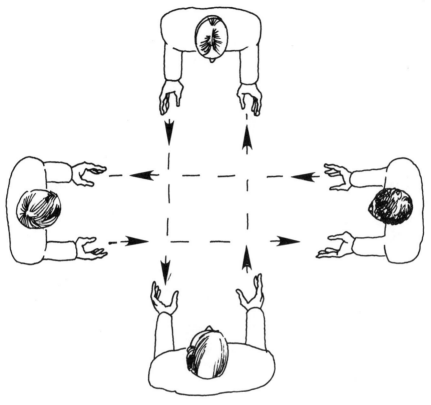

The Box.

time, A and B then pass their normal first throw. From that point A and B pass every other throw. C and D, on the other hand, do not start passing on their normal first throw. This means their pass is the fourth object, not the third. In other words, they throw one more object into their own juggling pattern before passing the first object across. After the first pass, C and D do a normal every other throw.

If you develop this pattern and keep it going, listen to the tempo. It is important that the juggling of each individual, plus the crossing of the clubs in the center, be in tempo.

The next step in the timing for the box is to learn the trick with everyone passing solid throws. There are two requirements toward accomplishing this feat. The first is that every juggler keep in *exact* tempo with everyone else. If the tempo of any juggler varies in the slightest, the objects will collide in the middle. The other requirement is the starting problem again. For a solids box, one set of passers must start one-half beat behind the others. In other words, if

A and B pass their first normal object, C and D's first passed object must follow one-half beat behind.

Instead of C and D starting by raising their right hands, with two objects in them, they instead raise their left hands with two objects in them. So, when A and B raise their right hands to start their juggle, C and D raise their left hands and start with a left hand downward motion and upward throw at the same time as A and B's right hand throws.

As C and D keep their cascade pattern going in tempo with A and B, watch the second throw from the left hand. When that objects gets to the right hand, pass it in tempo to your partner. From that point on pass solids.

Both A and B and C and D should be passing solids with the objects crossing in the center of the box. And remember, watch your timing!

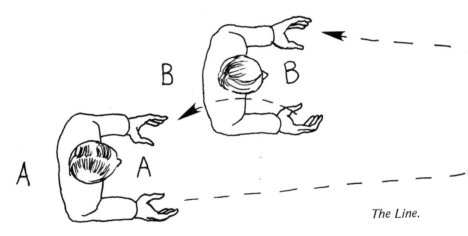

The Line.

The Line. Juggler A stands slightly out of line to the right of the middle juggler so that his passes to juggler C don't hit the middle juggler. Juggler A passes to C, C to B, B to A. The only difficult part of this is that B's objects *drop back* to A.

To accomplish the drop back throw, juggler B takes the object he would normally throw forward in a passing pattern and with the same hand and timing throws it up and back over his right shoulder. As the object goes over his shoulder, it should travel diagonally leftward so that it lands in juggler A's left hand. If you are doing drop backs with clubs, jugglers say the club is thrown a "double" turn. Actually, the club spins one and one-half times.

Right And Left Feed. As in a normal feed, the leader faces two other jugglers. However, in the right and left feed, the leader is passing solids with both of the other jugglers at the same time.

The leader's right hand is throwing every object to A, while his left hand is throwing every object to B.

Before going on, study the diagram and you will see that the leader as well as juggler B must be able to do a reverse passing pattern with control. Once the leader and B can control a reverse passing pattern, the group is ready to begin work on the right and left feed.

All of the jugglers start at the same time with two objects in the right hand, one in the left. From this point on, everyone's timing is different. First, the leader throws the first normal passing throw from his right hand to juggler A. Then he throws the object in his left hand to juggler B. He then alternates, right to A, left to B, right

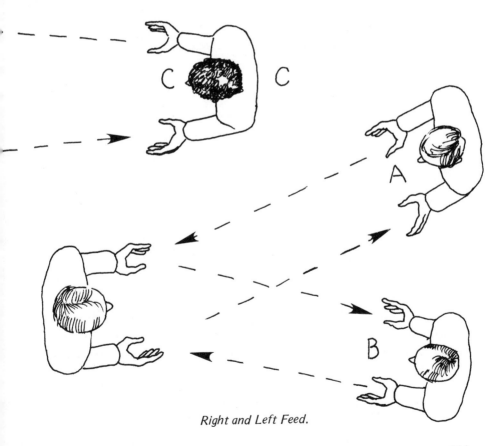

Right and Left Feed.

to A, left to B. This will cause the objects to cross alternately in front of the leader. The leader does not throw any throws between his own two hands once the passing begins.

Next, juggler A's first throw is the normal juggling start to the leader's left hand. From this point on, he throws solids to the leader's left hand.

Juggler B watches the second object thrown out of his right hand. When this object gets to the left hand, in a normal passing tempo, he throws it to the leader's right hand. From this point on, juggler B passes solid *reverse* direction throws to the leader's right hand.

The most crucial aspect of all these partner's patterns is that you can never be in competition. In fact, unless you are in complete unison, they won't work.

10 ADVANCED PATTERNS

The explanations of the juggling tricks in this chapter are very short. However the time it takes to learn them will be long. But just making an attempt at these difficult moves will help to improve your overall juggling skill.

SHOWER AROUND BACK

For this pattern you do a normal counter-clockwise shower except instead of throwing the balls from your left hand straight across sideways to your right, pass the balls behind your back.

To learn this trick, do the standard shower and then just pass one ball behind, and then continue the normal shower. When you pass the ball behind, your left hand goes behind your back and *places* the ball into your right hand. Once you understand how one ball is passed behind your back, you are ready to start learning the trick with each ball being passed behind your back.

BACKCROSSES-AROUND BACK EVERY THROW

Each ball, from both hands, is thrown around your back.

The first step in learning this trick is for you to learn "around your back" with either hand. Make sure each ball goes behind you and then up and over the opposite shoulder from the throwing hand. Another point to keep in mind is that people have a tendency to try to throw the balls behind their back too fast.

Backcrosses are a slow juggling move, so remember to keep a nice even normal juggling rhythm.

HEAD BALANCE

From a juggle you throw one ball up to a perfect balance on your forehead.

The main trick in learning this one is practice, lots of practice. The first thing you might want to practice is balancing a large broom stick on your forehead (see the chapter on balancing). After you can balance a large broom stick with complete control, work down to smaller and smaller sticks. After you can balance small sticks on your head, you are ready to start work on balancing a ball on your head, however, a big soccer ball, not a small juggling ball. Once you can balance a large ball, then try a small one.

Now you are ready to try throwing the ball to a balance from your hands.

Once you can do that, try the trick with smaller and smaller balls until you can do it with your normal juggling balls. And finally, learn to throw the ball up to a balance out of a three ball juggling pattern.

HAND, ARM, ELBOW BOUNCE

As your left hand holds one ball, the right hand keeps the other two balls bouncing off of the left forearm, left elbow, and back of the left hand in a continuous cycle.

Before you start on this trick, go back and read about the arm bounce. This is the first part of the trick. Ball number one thrown from your right hand bounces off of your left arm and goes back up to the right imaginary point. At this time two things happen. First, you throw ball number two out of the right hand toward your left arm. It must be thrown under ball number one but still in a normal cascade flight pattern.

Secondly, you must bring your left hand back so it touches your left ear. You will notice that your elbow is at about the same point where your forearm was before. So, as ball number two comes down, bounce it off of your elbow, back over to your right imaginary point.

Re-throw ball number one back over to the left in its normal flight pattern. Then move your left hand back up to approximately the same point where the elbow and forearm bounced their balls. Now bounce ball number one off of the back of your hand so that it travels back up to your right imaginary point. At this point you are ready to re-start the cycle. Throw ball number two to your forearm and you are on your way.

It is important that you realize ball number three, the one in the left hand at the beginning, is just clenched in your left hand, it doesn't come into play in this trick. And also remember that many variations of this order are possible.

REVERSE HANDS

What is unique about this juggling trick is the position of the hands and wrists during each catch on the normal cascade pattern.

Let your right hand hang down in front of your body. Straighten out your elbow and lift your hand palm up so your fingers are pointing to your left. Keeping your elbow locked and your palm up, rotate your hand counter-clockwise until your fingers are pointing to your right. This is the position your right hand will be in each time it catches the ball.

Your left hand will be in the same position except rotated clockwise.

Start with a normal cascade keeping your juggle very low. When one ball gets to your right hand, throw it a little harder than usual so it goes to the outside of the left arm. Now, turn your left hand around clockwise and catch the ball. As soon as you catch it, turn your left hand back around counter-clockwise and throw the ball back into the juggle with a normal throw.

Once you have mastered this, try it with the right hand. Then when you can do single catches with both hands, try and catch each ball with both hands in this position. Remember, only have your hands twisted when catching a ball, and straighten them around when you throw the balls.

OVER SHOULDERS SOLIDS

All of the balls from both hands are thrown behind you so that they go up and over your shoulders to your front, where they are caught by the opposite hand.

Go back and review what is meant by "over the shoulder" as compared to "around your back." In this trick, the balls go over your shoulders. Start with a ball thrown behind from your right hand. The ball should come up over your back and pass between your right shoulder and head on its path to the left imaginary point. Once the balls come over your shoulder, they cross to the opposite hand that threw them, which is why they reach the left imaginary point.

Once a hand throws a ball from behind your back, it must go back out in front of your body so that it can catch the next ball that it will carry behind your back to throw.

SOLIDS UNDER LEGS

Every ball thrown from every hand passes under one of your legs. All of the balls thrown from your right hand pass under your right leg. All of the balls thrown from your left hand pass under your left leg.

For this trick your juggling rhythm and basic cascade pattern remain the same as in "alternating under both legs." The only thing that is speeded up is the action of your legs raising and lowering. And it is very important that you throw all of the balls to their respective imaginary points.

THREE HIGH PIROUETTE

As you are juggling in a cascade pattern, quickly throw all three balls up in the air, turn in a pirouette, and then catch the balls back into a normal cascade juggle.

To begin work on this trick, go back and review two things. First, review "three high." Second, review "one high with a pirouette." Put both together and start practicing three high with a pirouette.

⑪ PERFORMING

A s soon as you show your juggling skills to a single person or to a group of people, you are a performer. And, as you develop your juggling, you may also want to evolve your performing. In this chapter I will introduce you to the basic fundamentals of performing.

ROUTINING

This is the order in which you put together your juggling tricks. This order will vary depending on individual ability and tastes. So, instead of listing a number of tricks, or groups of tricks in the order I would perform them, I am going to give you the guidelines I use to put together a routine.

Start by making a list of all the tricks you can do with the prop you are preparing the routine for. From this list pick out one starting trick, to start your routine.

Next, beginning with your starting trick, pick one trick at a time from your list of tricks. The prime consideration in choosing each new trick will be that the trick can be started out of the pattern of the last trick. Your tricks should flow together without having to stop or revert back to a basic cascade.

For example, if your starting trick is "two balls over your right shoulder," as the two balls come over your shoulder, the next trick you pick should be one that has two balls in front of your body, such as "one center-two out" or "stuck behind your back."

If you cannot mentally figure out which tricks flow into the next ones, get your juggling balls out and try all of the possibilities until you find the easiest one for you.

Every so often in a routine you will come to a point where you

Performing

cannot flow from the last trick into the next one. At these points a very effective transitional device is to simply do another start. For example, say you have just done a reverse cascade and the next trick you want to do in your routine is "stuck behind your back." Since it is very difficult to go from a reverse cascade to "stuck behind your back," you could catch two balls in your right hand, do a "two balls under your right leg" start, throw a left hand ball high and then go to "stuck behind your back."

Keep in mind that the last trick in each of your routines should be a trick that members of your audience like. Save your big audience pleaser trick for the end of your routine.

Variety and contrast in tricks can help keep up your audience's interest. For example, if your first trick is one where your juggling props are thrown very high, your next one could be more interesting if it was done with your juggling props thrown very low. Or, if you do a juggling trick where your hands are making hardly any movement at all, try the next trick with your arms making exaggerated movements.

PRESENTATION

You have now prepared your individual routine, but the next question is how should you handle yourself and your props to get the maximum effect out of that routine.

Practice. This is the foundation of a good routine. It is obvious that if you are constantly straining throughout all of your routines you will have little time to concentrate on producing the maximum effect.

Practice your individual routine and your total show in exactly the same order each day until you can do it with ease. Don't just practice individual tricks or routines. Practice the total routine and show so your muscles are at ease making one trick flow into the next.

I once knew a would-be juggler who practiced several individual prop routines at different times during the day. Then one day he was asked to do a show in which he did all of his routines right after each other. He felt he had the routines down cold, and he did know all the *individual* routines. But as a whole routined show he had never tried it. His first routine went well but he strained through the second, and the third was disastrous. His body was used to approaching each routine fresh without fatigue. However, as he put all of them together his muscles were not fresh, so consequently his routines got worse.

Movement. Most beginning jugglers forget to incorporate body movement into the movement of their juggling. Think about movement and try to work it into your juggling routines. Top jugglers are familiar with the basics of dance, mime, music, drama, and possibly comedy, depending on their total presentation. Study different types of movement and work it into your juggling routine.

Prop Stands and Assistants. It is of absolute importance that the juggler not fumble around as he is changing from one prop to the next. This can destroy the effect of the tricks.

Arrange your props in the order you will use them. Or, if you use an assistant to hand you the props, make sure they are arranged in an order that will guarantee that you are brought the right prop at the right time.

Appearance. Everything you wear or handle will communicate some impression to your audience. If you are a serious juggler in the traditional sense, your costumes should be neat and trim, your props should be decorated neatly with a conservative decoration. The person who is trying to be a serious juggler does not communicate that fact when he uses juggling clubs that are painted a variety of ultra bright fluorescent colors.

Make your total act reflect the character you want to be when you are juggling. If you want to be a witty comedy juggler, your costume should prepare your audience for that type of presentation. If you come out in a traditional circus juggler's glittery vest, that would not communicate comedy to the audience. However, if you come out in bright colored plaid sports jacket with one brown shoe and one black shoe, that tells the audience "this guy's a little funny." Instead of your prop stand being a nicely decorated box, maybe it's a trash can. Instead of using serious background music, you use light comedy music. Instead of juggling clubs you juggle toilet plungers.

Put simply, decide what kind of juggler you want to be during your act and then make your total act reflect that decision.

Entrances, Bows, and Exits. The way in which you execute these basics can easily make or break your total routine.

After you have been introduced and before you start your juggling, you need to acknowledge the audience's response to your introduction. You could come walking in and go to the front of your performance area and bow. Or you could simply walk on and say "hi" or "thanks." If you have difficulty with this get advice from drama teachers, books, or professional theater performers.

Always thank your audience when they applaud one of your tricks or routines. When you acknowledge them with the nod of your head or a "thank you," look directly at them and speak directly to them.

When I was first performing as a juggler, Bill Talent, a seasoned juggler from the days of vaudeville, explained the humbleness with which a performer should make his exit from the stage, using his exit to build applause, not kill it. He said after you have finished your last trick, and then taken a quick but sincere bow, you should begin to exit. If you simply turn and run off, the applause will end early because you are no longer on the stage. So, what you want to do is begin to walk off slowly, not turning your full side or back to the audience, but making sure they can see your face. If the applause continues with enthusiasm, stop periodically and nod your head with a "thank you." Make your total exit as the applause begins to diminish, and make sure you get off before it dies.

SHOWMANSHIP

This is the ability to make a trick seem more than it really is. The traditional example of showmanship in juggling is the *prepared* miss of a difficult trick to heighten the suspense of making the trick in the end.

Not an Accident. Showmanship is not an accident. You have to plan and experiment and fail before you will develop your own style of showmanship. You will know when you are beginning to develop it by listening to your audience. Listen for the points in your performance that get the most enthusiastic applause. Once you determine those points, analyze them and find out why they like them. Try all different kinds of approaches, always working to reach out and grab the audience's interest. Once you begin to do that with one or two tricks, work on other tricks until you can get results with your total routine.

Watch Other Performers. Watch other jugglers, other variety acts, and other performers in general. See what you and the audiences like about these performers and then work to bring out these techniques and qualities in *your* performance.

When You Accidently Drop. Because the skill of juggling lends itself to dropping props, this is an area where many students of juggling begin to develop their first feeling for the need of showmanship. For that reason, I am going to go through several of my thoughts on how you should handle a drop.

The Art of Juggling

First of all, when you drop a prop, speed or exaggerated quick jerky movements in picking it up will not cover the fact that you missed the prop. In fact, these movements will make your audience even more aware of the fact that you made a mistake, and heighten your chances of making another miss. So, when you do drop a prop, look at it, look at the audience, let the prop come to a standstill on the floor, take a deep breath, pick up the prop, look at the audience, think about what your next move will be, and then begin juggling again. Be relaxed and take your time.

There are three specific comedy flares you can do to turn the miss to your advantage.

● Before picking up the prop, walk over to your prop stand and put on a large pair of gag glasses that are available from novelty stores. Then pick up the prop and continue on with your juggling.

● As soon as you miss one of your props, take off your hat, or a handkerchief from your pocket, or your shoe and keep on juggling using that item and the props you did not drop.

● When you miss, turn to the audience and say one of the following: "Obviously a defective prop," "Don't worry, that's part of my act. The part I didn't rehearse," or "It looks like I'm turning this act into a *floor* show."

These three items are included, not as a complete list, but to get you started as far as your individual thinking about what you should do when you drop a prop. Experiment with your *own* ideas until you find ones that your audiences like.

JUGGLING BITS

Following are sixteen proven bits of juggling business that audiences like.

Color Changing Rings. As you are juggling rings, they appear to change colors. To accomplish this feat you need to paint your set of rings so one side is one color and the other side is another color. Then as you are juggling, with your side to the audience, they will see only one color. Now as you catch the rings, catch them with your palm up, grab the ring, then turn it over. In other words, you catch the ring with your palm up and then turn the ring over by returning your hand to its normal throwing position. By doing this, you will change the side, and the color, of the ring facing the audience.

For maximum effect, learn how to turn the rings over with both hands. By so doing you will speed up the color change.

Rings Over Your Head. As you are juggling 3, 4, 5, 6, 7, or 8 rings, finish by putting the rings over your head, right-left, right-left, right-left, etc., so they come to rest around your neck. If you put the rings over your head with a little speed and enthusiasm, this is a very showy effect and it will come as a nice surprise to the audience.

Juggling Blindfolded. It is possible to juggle blindfolded, however several manufactured blindfolds that you can see through are available from magic supply houses.

Juggling Behind Your Back. Somewhere in a three ball routine you stop, catching two balls in your right hand and one in your left. Then you place both of your hands behind your back, where the audience cannot see them and make arm movements as if you were juggling behind your back. Actually you are simply holding the balls and moving your arms only.

Juggling Backwards. After one of your juggling tricks you ask the audience "Would you like to see the same trick done backwards?" When they say yes, turn your back to your audience and do exactly the same trick you did before.

Comedy Blindfold Juggling. As this effect begins, you are standing sideways to the audience and juggling blindfolded. When you stop juggling and turn toward the audience there is a big laugh, as there is a big hole in one eye of the blindfold, enabling you to see out.

Bouncing Handkerchief. After you have been juggling for a few minutes, take out a handkerchief and wipe your brow. Once you finish wiping your brow, throw the handkerchief down hard against the floor, whereupon it bounces up and you catch it in your coat pocket.

There are two gimmicks that make this trick possible. First, get a ball that bounces well and sew it into the center of a handkerchief. This will allow the ball to bounce up from the floor. Secondly, sew a wire oval into the top of your breast pocket so that the top of the pocket stays open. This will allow you to catch the handkerchief as it bounces up from the floor.

Eating an Apple. The basic idea is to juggle two balls and one apple. As you are juggling, slowly eat the apple until you are juggling two balls and an apple core.

In order to have the time to take a bite from the apple, you will need to throw one of the two balls you are juggling up in the air several feet, thus giving you time to take a bite from the apple.

Also there are many variations of the basic idea. You could juggle an apple, a fork, and a napkin. Some of the possibilities with this combination would be throwing the apple high in the air and as it comes down, hold the fork, point up, under it, thus catching the apple on the fork. Or, every time you take a bite of the apple you immediately wipe your mouth with the napkin. You could also juggle a cup, saucer, and donut. Or, two hot dog buns and a hot dog. Or, a candy bar, candy bar wrapper, and a napkin.

Parasol and Ball. The juggler opens up a parasol and begins spinning a small ball on it by rotating the parasol.

The ball is kept in balance on the parasol for some time, then as the audience begins to applaud, the juggler stops the spinning of the umbrella and takes his bow. The audience now laughs as they see the ball is held on the umbrella by a string.

Ball and String. As you are juggling, let a ball go as if to drop it on the floor. However, the ball swings back through your legs and then back up into your juggle.

The ball swinging through the slightly spread legs is caused by the fact that it is attached by string to your coat buttons.

Putty Balls. You begin by throwing one ball high and letting it bounce on the ground before you resume juggling. After doing this several times with each throw going a little higher, you announce that you are going to throw one to the height of the roof. You throw the ball way up, it comes down, but instead of bouncing, it *plops* on the ground.

Simply use a wad of white·putty for the last ball you throw way up in the air.

Ball On Nose. Throw a ping pong ball up in the air above your head, and as the ball comes down, catch it in a perfect balance upon your nose. However, as the audience begins to applaud your seemingly fantastic feat, you bow—with the ball "stuck" to your nose.

To get the ball to stick to your nose, completely coat it with rubber cement. Then put some rubber cement on the end of your nose. Once you have done this, simply throw the ball up so it will come down upon the rubber cemented end of your nose.

When doing this feat for an audience, it helps build the comedy element if you really pretend to balance the ball on your nose when it first lands there.

Medals. When you do a particularly good juggling feat, pull a medal out of your breast jacket pocket and leave it for everyone to see. Later in your routine, when you miss a trick, tuck the medal back in your pocket. Then when you again make a good trick, again bring out the medal. Later on when you make a really exciting trick, open up your coat revealing a great number of medals pinned to the inside of your jacket.

Cannon Balls. Announce that you are going to attempt the very difficult feat of juggling three cannon balls. You try but at first drop one of the balls on the stage where it lands with a thud. So you try again, and again you drop it with a thud. Pick the balls up and try one last time. This time you successfully get the balls going, however after a few seconds one ball is thrown too high. It goes up in the air and then comes down and bounces with a thud on your forehead. If presented right this is a great comedy bit.

To accomplish the feat, find two solid wooden croquet balls and one rubber ball of exactly the same size. Now paint all three balls a black cannon ball color. It is important that all of the balls look exactly the same. I think it is now obvious that first you drop the solid wooden balls, then the ball that bounces on your head is the rubber ball. To get the thud when the ball hits your forehead, click the two solid wooden balls you are holding in your hands together.

Comedy Cigar Boxes. Hold three cigar boxes in front of you at waist level. All of a sudden do a very fast version of the traditional three cigar box juggling routine, moving the two end boxes around without ever letting the center one drop.

Position for starting the cigar box routine.

The Art of Juggling

Just as the audience begins to appreciate your skill, you bow revealing that the center cigar box is fastened by a heavy wire to your belt buckle.

Tray of Glasses. Take a tray full of glasses on a long pole and begin pouring some liquid into the glasses. After you fill them, raise the pole and tray up in the air and balance on your chin. All of a sudden the whole balanced arrangement begins to fall in the direction of the audience. You catch the pole but it is too late for the glasses. They begin to fall and the liquid begins to cascade down toward the heads of the audience.

But the liquid that is coming down is confetti and the glasses are firmly attached by heavy fishing string to the tray, which is firmly attached to the pole, which you are holding well above the heads of the audience.

The only other explanation needed is that when you first poured the liquid into the *non*-transparent glasses which already contained the confetti, you used a "Magic milk pitcher" available at magic supply houses.

So far the tricks in this book have involved the juggling of balls. However, there are a great number of varied props you can use, many more than people realize. In this chapter I will introduce you to many of them. Since each juggler has traditionally constructed his own individual props, there is no standardization. You should use this chapter to experiment with different props until you find the ones that serve you best.

JUGGLERS WHO SELL PROPS

There are several individual jugglers who sell the juggling props they make. By writing to these individuals you can find out more about buying props. Also, you can write to the International Jugglers Association, or me in care of the publisher.

Here are the jugglers I know of who construct and sell juggling props:

- Claude Crumley, 3 N. 305 Cardinal, Addison, Ill. 60101.
- Brian Dube, 7-13 Washington Sq. N., Apt. 47 B, New York, N.Y. 10003.
- Jay Green, 10 W. 47th St., Room 1206, New York, N.Y. 10036.
- Jack Miller, 1895 N. Kansas Ave., Springfield, Mo. 65803.
- Stuart Raynolds, 2716 Silverside Rd., Wilmington, Del. 19810.

THE BASIC PROPS

Rings. The three considerations in juggling rings are size, construction and design.

Size will vary from juggler to juggler. I have seen rings with an outside diameter of anywhere from 10" to 16". However, most jugglers end up with an outside diameter of 12-13½".

Next in determining the size of ring you will construct is thickness of the body.

Averages seem to be 1¼-1¾". You can cut different size rings out of cardboard and experiment to find the body size that allows you to hold the rings comfortably. The final size consideration is thickness. If you are using your rings for juggling outdoors or for passing, you will probably want a thickness of from ½" to ¾". However, if you are doing numbers juggling with your rings, you will probably want a thickness of 1/16" to 1/8".

Once you have experimented with different sizes of rings, your next interest will be in figuring exactly what to make your rings out of. There are two basic materials you can use: wood or plastic. If you use wood, a veneer is usually best. Once you have cut the ring out, you can sand the edges and then wrap the ring with plastic tape. The tape will prolong the life of the ring.

If you are going to construct your rings out of plastic, it would be best to go to a large plastics supply house and explain that you wish to make juggling rings and then listen to the plastic people on the kind of plastic that would be best to make the rings out of.

Once you cut your rings, be sure to sand the edges. Then you will be ready to decorate them.

Rings are much more impressive and enjoyable to juggle when decorated.

Sticks. Juggling sticks are either pieces of doweling or pieces of wood that have been turned on a lathe. They can range in length from 12" to 24", although the average seems to be between 16" and 18".

Usually the handle end of these juggling sticks are from ¾" to 1¼" in diameter, but again it depends on your individual taste.

Stick Clubs. The following stick clubs fall between being a juggling stick and a juggling club.

Chair leg model. The basic items used to make one of these clubs are:

- 1-16" to 18" tapered solid wood table leg.
- 1-3" to 4" dime store solid ball.
- 1-3½" to 4½" stove bolt.
- 1 large washer to fit the stove bolt.

When you get the table leg there will be a metal bolt sticking out of the largest of the two ends. If you take this out with a pair of pliers, you will have a hold in the large end of the table leg. So, when you buy the 3½" to 4½" stove bolt (the size should be ½" longer than the diameter of the ball you buy) get a bolt with a diameter that will thread down into the hole in the large end of the table leg.

The only other thing you must do before assembling your club is to drill a hole all the way through the ball.

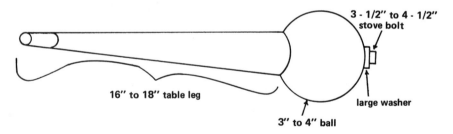

Stuart Raynolds Practice Stick. These practice sticks can also be purchased from Stuart Raynolds.

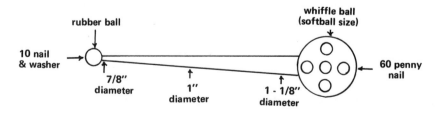

The Art of Juggling

Stuart Raynolds Practice Clubs. The following specifications may be used to make an inexpensive but excellent practice set of clubs with handles and knobs the same as standard American juggling clubs. These clubs are turned on a lathe from pine or basswood (1¾ x 1¾) stock.

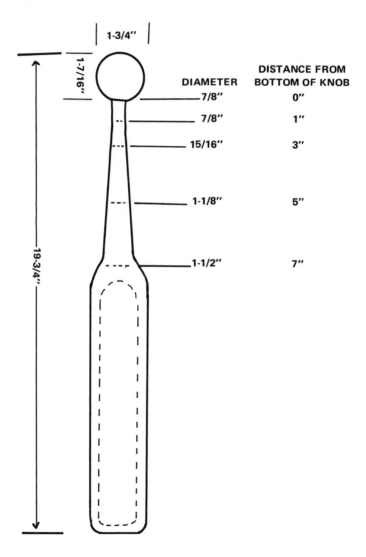

	DIAMETER	DISTANCE FROM BOTTOM OF KNOB
	7/8"	0"
	7/8"	1"
	15/16"	3"
	1-1/8"	5"
	1-1/2"	7"

Most important is the shape of the knob and the thickness and taper of the handle. With the two dimensions on the knob and the fine diameters on the handle, a good turner can reproduce this taper exactly. After turning these clubs, they should be sanded and then painted with a glossy enamel.

If you don't wish to personally make these practice clubs you can obtain them from Stuart Raynolds, 2716 Silverside Rd., Wilmington, Del. 19810.

Plastic Bottle Stick Club. To make this stick club take a dowel from 16" to 18" in length with a diameter from ¾" to 1¼". On the end of this dowel, slip over an old round *plastic* bottle.

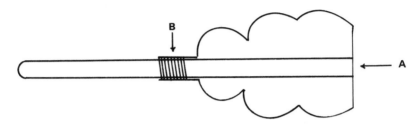

At point A, put a nail with a large washer on it through the plastic into the dowel. Then at point B, tape the plastic bottle onto the dowel.

Clubs. The first two methods of constructing juggling clubs are out of wood and fiberglass. Most of these clubs weigh somewhere between 6 and 14 ounces and are from 18" to 20" in length. Methods of construction are complicated, therefore, if you have an interest in producing either I would suggest that you write the individuals listed in the beginning of this chapter who make props.

The next method, the "cork club," would be started by turning a wooden handle out of a good hard wood.

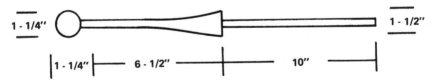

The dimensions given in the above drawing are given so you have an idea of size, however, there is nothing absolute about them as you, and only you will be able to decide what is just right for you.

Next obtain and glue several pieces of blocked cork together and turn them on a lathe so as to produce a club body.

By drilling a hole through the center of the body, you can slip the cork over the dowel end of the club handle.

Before slipping the cork over the dowel, spread a little glue on the dowel. When the whole cork club is together it should weigh somewhere between eight and 12 ounces.

The last method for constructing clubs is the European Method. Start by gathering the following:

- 1-lathe turned handle
- 1-lathe turned club end
- 1-3¾" circular piece of ¼" wood with a 3/8" hole drilled center
- 1-1 7/8" circular piece of ¼" wood with a 3/8" hole drilled in the center
- 1-piece of doweling 3/8" by 14" long
- 8-¼" x 1/8" x 12" bamboo strips
- 1-package of small nails
- 1-ball of strong string
- 1-bottle of good wood glue
- 1-roll of surgical tape
- decorative foil

Once you have gathered together the parts, assemble the two round pieces, the turned handle, the turned end, and dowel, being sure to glue everything in place with the wood glue.

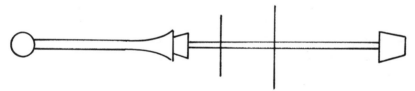

Next, tack the first bamboo strip down.

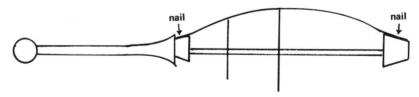

After putting down the first strip, continue on which the other seven bamboo strips, spacing them out evenly around the body of the club:

After spacing and then nailing the eight bamboo strips around, next wrap string around points A and B.

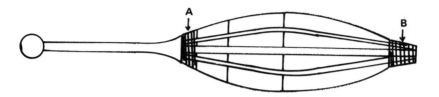

Wrap the string thickly but evenly. Once you tie the string off, rub glue all around it to give it strength.

Next, wrap the body of the club with surgical tape.

And finally, decorate the body with a foil paper.

You can also use small thin rattan doweling instead of bamboo strips.

Fire Torches. Fire torches can be very dangerous, so make sure you are a competent juggler before even beginning to think about juggling fire torches. And, once you do begin, make sure someone is close by who really knows how to put out a fire.

Method number one for fire torch construction is to take an old twirling baton, cut it down so it is from 18" to 21" in length, wrap strip asbestos material around it and then screw the ends of the asbestos into the baton so the whole end doesn't slip off.

As you use this fire torch, make sure that you periodically check the screws to see that they are secure.

Method number two for construction is turn a wooden club type handle, so that a 4½" piece of metal tubing fits over the end.

Next, wrap a three inch strip of asbestos material around the metal tubing and place the tube over the end of the handle.

Finally, run three nuts and bolts through the asbestos, metal tube, and wooden handle, thus securing the total torch together.

One last suggestion would be that you rivit the ends of the bolts after the unit is assembled, thus making sure that the fire torch will never fall apart on you.

VARIATIONS ON THE BASICS

If you understand the basic props of the traditional juggler, your next step in prop selection will be to find variations of the basics. The following is a quick, incomplete list of some of the possible variations. You can make up your own variations by thumbing through department store catalogs, or by visiting any of the larger toy stores. The limitations are only what you make them.

Ball variations: basketballs, marbles, apples, oranges, walnuts, eggs, handkerchiefs, etc.

Ring variations: hula hoops, life preservers, Christmas wreaths, bicycle rims, records, plates, tambourines, hats, etc.

Stick and club variations: tennis racquets, bats, banjos, guitars, knives, hammers, toilet plungers, horns, umbrellas, bottles, canes, etc.

Juggling three canes in a cascade will be very different from juggling three balls. You must learn that the cane has to make one turn when going from hand to hand. Each new object you work with is going to differ from balls, and it is good practice to start working with just one to get a feel for it before going with three. Eventually, you can try juggling three different objects.

⑬ THE BEGINNING: A New Essence

After more than 16 years of juggling, I am still beginning. I have achieved far more than I ever thought possible. I have a stable living condition, a healthy income and materially everything I could want.

Yet, the childlike thrill is still there each time I master a new trick. This is why I juggle. My performing, which has earned my living and reputation, which has taken me from the New York World's Fair to Disneyland to the "Wild Wild West" television show, is not the reason. The thrill of that has always been secondary to the sensation I get from learning a new trick in the privacy of my Illinois home with no audience, except my wife.

British writer Walter Pater wrote of this more than a hundred years ago. "Art comes to you proposing frankly to give nothing but the highest quality to your moments as they pass."

How many moments of how many lives pass at less than highest quality?

It may sound unlikely that an hour of daily juggling can positively affect the rest of your life. But it has and it does.

Juggling can halt the stagnation that negates so much of life. The juggler can go to it for refuge when life gets too difficult. He can use it for a boost when his motivation ebbs. He can use it as a relaxant when life becomes too charged. It offers the divisions that average life lacks.

It also strikes directly at an increasingly disturbing problem. While we are growing more in touch with space and technology, we are losing touch with our bodies. It actually frightens people to look in the mirror and see that they are growing old or getting fat. I've seen many people who are afraid even to catch a set of keys thrown to them. This is how unconfident some people are of their bodies. I believe that a prime reason for this is that, through years of neglect, a great many simply don't know themselves and what their capabilities are. The idea of actually putting one's body to any sort of test really scares some people.

A half hour of daily juggling puts your mind more in tune with your body. You probably have discovered this as you have developed, and will continue to discover as you continue to develop. The knowledge you gain of your physical self surprises most people, but more surprising is the realization of how little you previously knew.

This lack of self-knowledge is at the root of many personality difficulties. Lack of confidence, despair, over-indulgence and many other instabilities often stem from a lack of understanding of the physical body.

A strenuous session of football does not put you in tune with your body. You are too busy thrashing it and testing it to gain any real understanding of it. Jogging has many benefits, but gives only a very limited exposure to your sense of coordination. Meditation does not involve the body enough to let you understand it.

A session of juggling, though, involves all parts of the body and, in solitary practice, hastens this understanding.

It is true that knowledge is power, and the knowledge of oneself yields the greatest power. Personal experience has shown me that the power gained through juggling increases confidence and creativity in all aspects of life.

This is why I'm not spending my life in a routine job which I don't particularly enjoy, but instead own a company called The Idea Machine Inc., which deals with creative inventions.

Just how much juggling can accomplish wasn't fully revealed to me until several years ago when, because of an accident, I was unable temporarily to juggle. I had seriously injured my hand and was told I probably would need to have a finger amputated. Not realizing my involvement with juggling, the doctor didn't understand why I reacted so frantically. If I had merely taken it hard, as most people might, it would have seemed normal. It's not pleasant losing a finger, but there are still nine good ones (more than most people need anyway).

I protested enough, the finger was spared and today it operates fine. But the whole experience served to show me that I was more than just attached to juggling. I was addicted.

Juggling is the sort of addiction that can save you. Dr. William Glasser wrote a book on this called *Positive Addiction*, in which he said that addiction need not be the sinking self-defeating horror we often take it to be. This is negative addiction; there is also positive addiction. Opposite in name, it is also opposite in effect. Positive addictions are habits that develop strength, power and creativity.

Besides showing me this addiction, and the importance of it in my life, the experience with my injured hand also made me more aware of how unlimited juggling really is. With just one usable hand, I was able to develop tricks I never would have developed otherwise.

No matter what you believe your physical limits or handicaps to be, if you have hands you can juggle. And you will find that your limits really aren't so limiting, or your handicaps so handicapping.

I've learned that people are intrigued by the *act* of juggling. Talking with members of various audiences over the years, I've found that many feel very removed from it. They often seem in awe, as though I possess some sort of magical abilities.

The abilities aren't magical. Many of them aren't even very difficult. They come with practice (as opposed to work) and are available to any who are interested.

I believe juggling is the most unlimited sport there is. New tricks are invented all the time. Few people who develop beyond the basic pattern ever feel the need to quit. They are pulled instead by the need to learn and create.

Whether you've mastered all the tricks in this book or if you're still working on the basic cascade, you are nevertheless a beginner. Where to go from here is not a question you will have. It is rather a decision you will make, probably not too consciously.

The specific path you take cannot be predicted. It is different for everyone. Most start with the basic cascade, but soon veer off in separate directions, as new and different tricks appeal to them and as they invent their own variations and combinations.

The juggling population has been limited by a mass misunderstanding, but is potentially as boundless as the sport itself. It has been a slow war against an unfair reputation. The *Encyclopedia Britanica* points out that ". . . it was not until the 19th Century that the juggler came into his own in the circus and music hall." There is no reason to stop there. Maybe this will be a new beginning.

What I have presented in this book is a composite of juggling. It can be used as a reference book to relearn certain tricks or to learn new ones. It is not meant to be followed step by step, cover to cover.

Hopefully, you will pick it up and put it down many times. Each time you finish a segment of it, you begin the sport all over again. And as you reach new plateaus, this book will take on different values for you.

You've made a profitable investment. This book, like juggling, cannot become obsolete.